Bob,
enjoy!

Tall IN THE Saddle

LORNE A. MAULL

Ride proud
Throw an honest loop
Be a good friend

Lorne A Maull

ISBN

978-1-4602-5318-2 (Hardcover)

978-1-4602-5319-9 (Paperback)

978-1-4602-5320-5 (eBook)

Produced by:

FriesenPress

Suite 300 – 852 Fort Street

Victoria, BC, Canada V8W 1H8

www.friesenpress.com

Distributed to the trade by The Ingram Book Company

Table of Contents

DEDICATION

This book is dedicated to my wife Diane who has ridden beside me for nearly 50 years, and to my family who have encouraged me to write and to record stories for future generations. May we keep alive some of the tales of our "Old Wild West."

Lorne A. Maull

INTRODUCTION

I was born and raised during the depression on an isolated small farm on the Canadian Prairies. I rode horse back four miles to a one-room school for nine years, until it closed.

Being part of the work force at a very early age, I knew what Heritage Farming was all about. Towards the end of the war there was no money, and I learned to fix and repair everything.

Over the years I have made wonderful friends many of whom were four legged. None of my dogs, horses or hired men ever worked for me, they worked with me.

My life journey has been interesting, in that I was born early enough, and lived in a remote enough area, that there was still a lot of "Wild" left in our West.

Don't let fear and common sense stop you from saddling up and riding along with me, and sharing the happenings of the 7M Running Bar.

Lorne A Maull
60 Years a Rancher & Storyteller of the 7M-

on, and as I learned never to let them make me cry, it seemed to take some of the fun out it for those mean bastards.

A major happening at our school was the hanging. Boy did this story spread like a stubble fire over a wide area, and became very exaggerated.

I was an innocent bystander, but still involved.

There was a sand pit south of the schoolhouse were I used to play and kind of stay out of sight and mind of the big mean kids. This day one of them came over and yells at me.

"Get your halter rope, we are going to hang Snoose".

Now Snoose was always chewing snuff, and would spit into his inkbottle during class. Thus the nickname. I ran and got my rope from the coatroom and headed for the barn where the event was to take place. I never did know what the crime was, but they had him standing on an old bucket under a rafter with his hands tied behind his back. One of the big boys put my rope around his neck and then over the rafter. I had never seen a hanging before so made myself small and unnoticed under a manger, and watched.

About this time I guess old Snoose thought this was getting out of hand. He gave out the most God-awful screech and made a jump for freedom. It kind of sounded like when my old dog would check out the tenderness of the hams on one of my dad's feeder hogs. On Snoose's way off the bucket, with his hands tied, there was no way to protect himself. He bounced off the manger and hit his head on the heelpost, and a spike was sticking out and gave him a huge gash on his head.

There he laid crying in the horse poop and dust. Two of the older girls came running to see what was happening. They took one look and grabbed him by his bib overalls, hauled him out of the horse poop, and headed for the teacher. She got him in the school and cleaned up. Then the lecture started, from a calm tone to a high-pitched scream, and even a few curses. I distinctly remember her tapping my rope on her desk. I was thinking here comes another casualty of the war…

Then my brain started working---because I could count to fifty by then. I knew that it was twenty steps to the door. I figured that if I could just make it to the steps, and jump onto my old pony....

Escape was in view. Then on second thought I'd seen this teacher hit a soft ball and run bases. I just knew she could pass my horse on a race to the gate. So I just sat and hoped for a painless death.

I guess that she realized that a little grade one could not have plotted a crime of this magnitude. She gave me my rope back so I could ride home that night when school was over.

The next day after the so-called neck tie party, all the parents arrived plus the school inspector. He drove a nice big car and acted like a third cousin to God. Snoose was right up at the front of the schoolroom. I think he felt pretty proud of all the attention he got, as he had never been at the head of the class before.

There was a lot of yelling, shouting, and blaming. Finally a big Norwegian lady said, "Ya lets all have some coffee and cool down a bit, it's just a kid's prank". Everyone calmed down and coffee was served. The people of the district went home thinking that everything was fine again.

Some of the older boys soon quit school to help with the harvest, while others just decided that they had enough education.

And for me the beatings almost quit.

So went the first half year of my formal education.

Koko & I at Setting Sun School

CHAPTER 2
DREAMS OF BEING A COWBOY

One Sunday morning as we were driving, I noticed all the bikers, with their fancy ten speed bikes. They had lights, horns, GPS's and God knows what else on their bikes. Of course the riders had flashy spandex with matching helmets and gloves.

We then drove past an outdoor riding arena, where some very young girls were taking riding lessons. I happen to know that the parents of these girls are spending copious amounts of money to have their little riders reach the level 3 of English Riding, and or Western Riding, and for each course you need a different horse. Most of these little cowgirls live in the city, and don't have any hope of ever owning a horse, so pay huge fees for lessons, horse rent, and arena fees.

Seems strange when you think of so many people in need right here in our society.

While driving along I just had a flash back to when I was a little boy. Now that is a long time ago, but kids have not changed. We were very poor and had to make our own entertainment, with NO money. We desperately wanted to be cowboys, but being poor the old bib overalls and lace up shoes were the style for most of the homesteaders. To this day I would sooner fight than wear those bib overalls. However being poor did not curb our imagination. We would ride the pail bunter calves, or skim dinks, as they were also called. We would imagine that we had fancy spurs, and that we were raking the hair off of those calves from the shoulders to hips.

We were hoping that the judge would notice our arm in the air, and our graceful style. Sometimes you would dismount so nicely, and bow to the cheering imaginary crowd. Other times you would get bucked off, and have to wipe the calf manure off your hands and face. These calves were in a small corral and soon were broken to ride. They would just stand still and take all the fun away from the little cowboy.

One day my dad arrived home with several new calves that he had just bought from a neighbor. They were from a rancher, and they were wild. He had also picked up the mail, and our cousins from Edmonton were coming to visit us for a couple days. Excitement was running pretty high. When they finally arrived wearing brand new Levi cowboy pants, my heart really went down. But then I had heard that "cloths did not make a man," so I felt some better. Plus we had been planning a big rodeo in our old corral for some time.

The next day we went to work building a little runway and a chute. It took just about every loose board on the farm, but finally it was done to our boyish standards.

Our one cousin was too small to ride, so we made him a little seat on the lean-to of a calf shed. He was to be the announcer, and had a disk blade hanging on a wire. He had a big hammer so that when the ride was over he could hit the disc blade and make a big Boing. His megaphone was an old cardboard box rolled up and tied together with binder twine.

We chased these wild calves around the corral for about twenty minutes before we finally got one into the chute. We put a rope around its heart girth, with the milk cow's old bell for added buck.

I don't know how I got nominated to ride this wild beast but the announcer bellowed.

"Out of chute number six comes that all around cowboy Lorne Maull from Setting Sun, on the famous Bucking Bull Buzz Bomb."

I don't know why he said number six as we only had one chute!

Whether or not the chute boss cracked the gate or if Buzz Bomb decided that he'd had enough rodeo fame, but he broke out of that chute like a rocket, wearing part of the chute around his neck.

I lasted two jumps, and on my way down he kicked me on the side of the head.

There was no "Cowboy Up" then.

I just got up and headed for the house with the blood running down my face and bawling like a baby.

My brother was running along beside me saying, "are you dead, are you dead?"

Mother stopped rolling her piecrust and calmly sat me down on a kitchen chair. She started to wash the blood and calf manure off my head.

There was a perfect imprint of the calf's hoof embedded in my skull, that took years to grow out.

While she was doing this, in came little Bobby wailing like a Banshee. Mother asked, "Where are you hurt?"

He just sobbed. "I didn't get to hit the disk, and hear it go BOING"

For some reason that rodeo never caught on, and was my dad ever mad. We were told to, "leave those so and so calves alone". He made us tear down the stampede corrals, even our chute # 6, and put every board back.

It was a sad day for those little cowboys to see their future destroyed.

Chapter 3
The Younger Years

Life in school got better as the years went on. I wasn't the smartest pupil in the world but I could learn. The best part of it all was that I started to grow and by the time that I was twelve, I had reached a height of six feet.

There was one neighbor lady who was very short. Every time she met me she would always say in a loud voice, "aren't you ever going to stop growing?" Being terribly shy she would just do it to embarrass me. She is now dead, but to this day I still dislike her. The saying was that she was so short that her brain was too close to her rear end. (I didn't always say it quite that way.)

I was now riding a thoroughbred horse to school named Banner who had been to slow for the racetrack. I had bought him on time from my uncle for $45.00, and my payments were $ 5.00 per month. On the way home from school we always had horse races and Banner had no trouble winning against the other school ponies who were often old retired work horses. I was still riding bare back.

In the winter I would hunt coyotes. Banner could put me up on a coyote in less than half a mile. I owned a bolt action nine shot 22 Savage Rifle that I had bought when I was nine. If you missed your shot at the coyote, you had to hold the reins in one hand, brace the gun on that forearm, and reload with your other hand. All the time gripping to hang on with your legs on the dead run. Banner would never step on a coyote no matter what, nor did he ever fall with me on board. This may all sound rather boring, but remember I was only 12 years old.

After I skinned the coyote out I would turn the hide inside out and stretch it on a board to dry, which took a couple weeks. When dry, you took it off the board and turned it back right side out. The Municipal District paid a bounty of $2.00 a hide. You would take the hide to the M.D. Office, where they would split the ears on the coyote, and give you your $2.00. Then you'd rush home and wrap up the hide to send it to The Hudson's Bay Fur Company to get another $2.00.

You waited and waited to receive this big check in the mail.

Things were pretty routine now. The one thing that I had learned from all the beatings in my early school years, was to hate a bully. In the later years I have been in quite a few dust ups to help the underdog.

Another big money maker in those years was collecting crow and magpie eggs and feet. Most kids would keep them in a can or jar. Rodgers Golden Corn Syrup pails were ideal because they had a bail and a lid. There were always lots of them around as we used them to take our lunches to school…sometimes they served a dual purpose. After a few warm weeks in May of collecting you would take the can to school for the teacher to count. You can image the smell when she would take the lid off the syrup pail. You would tell her how many eggs, and feet that you had collected. She would watch you very closely, and see if you looked a little shifty. Then she would smile and say, "That looks about right" and pay you. Later she would be reimbursed by the M.D.

We may have cheated a little, but for three cents per egg, and five cents for the odd extra a pair of feet, I don't think that we hurt the taxpayers too much. If you got lucky you could try to blow out the eggs that were due to hatch, and retrieve a pair of feet as well. As kids we thought this was big money, but I don't think that it came close to paying for the torn clothes from climbing the trees to get at the nests.

We would play ball, fox and goose, and use cardboard boxes to slide down the hill in the schoolyard. The best game off all I thought was Horse Turd Hockey. In the winter you would go out and clear the snow off a level spot in the schoolyard. We then would search the school barn and yard for the right specification horse turd for a puck. Then it was to the Poplar and Willow Bluffs to cut just the right stick, with the correct curve or knob, to be able to hit with. These trees where frozen and were very hard to cut with your jack-knife. Every farm boy in those days carried a jackknife.

The goalie would usually use old magazines, or newspapers to wrap around his shins and knees, then hold them on with rubber sealer rings that he had snitched from his mother. No one had ever heard of using a jock strap or can in those days. … but nobody ever ended up with a high squeaky voice, and they all grew up to have families, so I guess that no permanent damage was done. We did sport periodic black eyes and the odd split lip.

Life never seemed dull in those days as we made our own fun and nobody seemed to get hurt. I never could run too fast but I was big and strong and could hit a soft ball a mile. One time our senior ball team asked if I would play with them at a sports day. You can bet that the buttons on my shirt popped off, and I felt that I was all grown up now. A real man at 13 years.

As I remember we didn't win the tournament that day but in the one game I hit three home runs and made a couple of fantastic catches on shortstop. After the sports day I was able to stay late for the Dance. I was standing by the hall door, and in comes several of my teammates. They grabbed my arm and said, "come on, let's go outside and have a drink of beer to celebrate those three homeruns."

I had never had a drink of alcohol before. They popped the caps, toasted all around and tipped them up. When the beer hit my throat and stomach, it's a good thing it was dark, because I coughed and gagged, and my eyes watered. I checked around to see if it wasn't some trick, because the ball players really seemed to like it. They all went for a second but I left in a hurry and couldn't see the pleasure in that brown bottle.

During those younger days there was a neighbor boy who used to ride over and visit us. Now I won't say he was the cause, but we seemed to get into a lot more trouble when he came. One day he came over with a box of rifle shells and smokes. We didn't have a rifle so we went out behind the hill for a smoke and to set off these shells. We would lay the shell on one big rock and hit it with another rock.

It was getting dark and the fireworks were great. To this day I don't know why we didn't get killed. After the twenty or so shells were all exploded, and a couple more smokes, we decided to wrap our arms around each other and roll down the high hill like a barrel. This was a faster and bumpier ride than any midway you could imagine. When we hit the bottom I was puking and was probably as green as the grass. My world was going around as I staggered back to the house, just hoping that I would die.

I remember my mother saying that it must have been something that I ate, but I'm sure she darned well knew, because I must of smelled like a smoke house.

Another time Carl came over we went riding, to just enjoy the freedom of the county and to just be boys. This time my parents weren't home, and unbeknown to his mother, Carl had brought along his old Single Shot 22 and of course a box of smokes. This old gun wouldn't always discharge, so he carried a wrench in his pocket to give the hammer a little tap, to help the firing pin work when necessary. His mother, who was a widow, discovered that he had taken the gun, and began to burn up the old party telephone lines trying to find us. We didn't know what a commotion that we were causing as we had ridden a long way, and it was getting late. It was a bright moonlight night, and you could see fairly well.

Riding through a field of oat stooks, we saw something that looked a lot like a bear. We pulled our horses to a stop, and tried to decide whether it was a bear or not.

Carl, not wanting anything to charge us, got out his wrench, loaded his rifle and hammered six shots into this thing.

It didn't move so we rode up to check it out. That old stook never had a chance. It had been shot dead in the center bundle. With that adventure over we said goodbye and each rode our own direction home. I never did hear how Carl made out but I know that I sure caught a lot of hell when I got home about midnight.

My pet Magpie

CHAPTER 4

WELLS

Today we take our water for granted. You go to the tap, turn it on and have a nice cold drink, or relax in a nice warm bath. You then go outside and turn the sprinkler on the lawn or garden. You open a plastic bottle of water, never dreaming of the hardships our forefathers had to just find water enough to survive. They also had to have enough water for their livestock.

Our family had dug a well that was eighteen feet deep, and about four feet square. It had been hand dug many years before I arrived on the scene, and was used for many years. My dad built the cribbing as they went down. There was a 2 by 4 at each corner, and shiplap was nailed to make a square box-like structure. They dug the hole with a pick and shovel and pushed down the cribbing as they went, adding sides as they went down. This meant that the well had to be dug a little bigger than the cribbing, so it would settle down into the hole as you dug.

On many of the homesteads the men dug, and the women pulled up the dirt in buckets on a rope. Can you imagine the amount, and the weight of the shovelfuls of dirt hauled up by the bucketful, and dumped out on the ground, away from the well?

When the well became deep there was the deadly risk of running out of oxygen. A ladder to escape was built on the inside of the cribbing, as it went down. Some would take a pet canary, or a captured sparrow in a cage down the well with them. If the bird passed out, it was time to get out of the well, or you could be next. Others would take a lit lantern down. If it started to flicker, or went out, the oxygen supply was gone, and you had little time to crawl out.

I remember my dad telling of how many days they had dug, and there was still no sign of water. That night they were totally discouraged and left their tools in the bottom of the well. The next morning, much to their surprise the water vein had broken loose during the night, and there was four feet of water in the bottom of the well. To this day there is still a pickaxe and a shovel in the bottom of that well.

There was no such thing as pressure treated lumber in those days. Our well was just tongue and groove shiplap. The water would rot the wood, so that about every five years it had to be repaired and or replaced.

I remember how important it was for the pioneers to have water. Many dug their wells before settling on a piece of land permanently. Sometimes three or four wells would be dug before hitting water on a homestead. The livestock were situated near the well, and often the house was quite a distance away. The women would have to carry water for bathing, cooking, and washing. Often there was an endless supply of diapers, all to be washed by hand.

If there was a cloudburst or heavy rainfall, the water would likely leak in the side of the well, and wash in dirt, silt and other filth. You would repair the cribbing then bail out the water as much as you could. Then you would crawl down the well with your bucket and shovel, to try to bucket out all the dirt, silt etc. Again you needed someone up top to pull it up on the rope and empty the bucket of slop. You were also working against the natural inflow of clean water. If you weren't working fast enough the inflow would get ahead of you. Even with a good crib, about once a month or so someone would have to bail out frogs, gophers, and mice that were floating on top of the water. This you would do with a rope and a pail.

As things became more modernized we bought a wooden pump, which had a drain hole below the frost line. Sometimes in extremely cold weather the pump would still freeze up. You would have to bring a big teakettle of boiling water from the house and pour it down the pump to thaw the cylinder. As the leathers wore out in the pumps they lost their prime, and you had to pour water down the pipe, nearly every time you wanted water. Thus the old term "Priming the Pump."

There was a platform built onto the cribbing, at about eight to ten feet. This was used to store cans of cream until they could be shipped. In the winter it kept the cream from freezing, and in the summer they were chilled so the cream did not spoil. These were either five or eight gallon cream cans that were lowered and raised on ropes, after each milking. Often meat and other perishables were also hung down the well. Mice had a bad habit of falling, or crawling down the wells. They would drown, and if the lids weren't on the cream cans, they would end up in them, so had to be fished out before the cream could be shipped. The cream was our grocery money, and I don't ever remember my mother throwing away any cream, just because of a mouse. I just hope that she didn't feed us any, but guess that "what the mind doesn't know the heart doesn't grieve".

We had never heard of e-coli in those days. You either drank the water or died of thirst! The water trough was right beside the well. There was a short spout made of wood, or if you had a few pennies, a piece of metal pipe was purchased. The cows and horses would crowd around the water trough, as there were no fences to keep them away from it. Of course there was always a big mess around the well.

We had a big Clydesdale horse named Don. He would just clamp his mouth over the spout and drink. As a kid on the pump handle I often got so tired just trying to fill him up. He wouldn't let go of that spout until he was full.

Later somebody invented a boring machine that made a hole three feet across, that could bore down about 100 feet. At first they used either an oxen or horse to go around in a circle to drive the auger. Later they had motors to drive them. They needed men to shovel away the dirt that was being augured up. Tongue and grove lumber was treated, and installed vertically in a circle, down the well. These wells were very dangerous, and if something or someone ever fell in, they were lost forever.

We had a neighbor who had a brand new bored well. He used to gamble and had a craps game at his house, which had lasted well into the night. The day after one of these late evenings a litter of baby pigs was missing. He was sure that one of his gambling buddies had stolen them. Quite sometime later he began to pump up pig hair and other parts, so then knew where his litter of pigs had gone. This fellow had six kids and they all grew up to be big and strong, with no apparent ill effects.

Another story is about two fellows digging a well with a shovel and a windless to pull up the mud. The outfit came apart about half way up the well, and the full bucket of mud hit the guy down the well on the head.

Everything seemed fine, and the work continued. In the middle of the night, the victim went goofy, and got up and tried to kill his partner with a butcher knife, chasing him down the road. When the chase arrived at the neighbors they were able to subdue him, and took him to the hospital. Unfortunately, although the man recovered he was never mentally the same again.

When my parents could finally afford a drilled well, we witched this well with a green V shaped willow stick. In our family my mother and I were the only ones capable of this talent. The water driller thought that there might be a shortage of water so he perforated the 6 -inch casing every two feet so as to catch each water vein. This worked great, except that before every weather disturbance, when the barometric pressure would fall, the silt and sand would seep into the pipe through these holes. We would get sand in our house plumbing, and this would plug things up. Later we had a new driller come, and he installed a 5-inch pump inside of the old six-inch casing. They went down 180 feet, and hit a rock. They ground through this for three days, and then all of a sudden the drill stem just dropped and they were through the rock ledge. They hammered the pipe down, and sealed it off at the rock formation. There was no more sand, and we watered over 1200 head of livestock at this well, and always had enough water pressure in the house as well. This was done over 60 years ago and is still pumping. There must be a huge lake underground at this location. An added benefit was that the well contained natural fluoride, to enhance bone and tooth structure.

If you drilled and got a flowing well, or artisan well, you were very lucky. If there was enough water pressure you could have running water in your house, and you never needed a pump, or pressure tank. However, if it was weak, the wintertime was a problem with ice build-up all over the yard. The livestock would be slipping on it and could easily break a leg.

I have seen many different water systems, the most unusual was a sand point pipe driven horizontally into a hillside, which flowed like a tap.

In the Peace River country you couldn't drill a good well so the water supply was dependent on water holes to catch the run off you preserved for year round use. A friend of mine homesteaded up there, and he always said that you slapped the water really heard, with the palm of your hand, and dipped a bucket of water out in a hurry. This scattered all the tadpoles, and the water bugs away, and you got fairly clean water,

Today water is still a very precious resource, but available to all in many different forms.

The next time you nonchalantly take a drink of water, just think of the history of this substance known as Adams Ale!

Old Hay Rake & Ginger

CHAPTER 5
HOMESTEADER FARMING

When I was young, the size and number of your feed stacks dictated the number of cattle that you could feed for the winter. Where I grew up you could count on feeding your livestock for at least 150 days each year. It would take two men to feed an 80 cow heard, depending on how far you had to haul the hay, and how cold the weather was. When the temperature went below -40 degrees each animal would need about half again as much feed, just to maintain their body temperature.

Some of my early memories are of my dad cutting hay with the five-foot power mower pulled by Don and Ben, our two faithful horses. The meadow was two miles from home so dad would hook the horses to a wooden wheeled wagon with a hayrack on it. He would tie Barney and Ribbon, our other team, behind the hayrack. You could only work horses so many hours, as pulling the mower was very hard work. When we stopped for a lunch break we would change teams, take out the mower sickle and sharpen it with a hand sharpening stone, and grab a bite of packed lunch to eat. We used to keep our drinking water cold by placing it in a gallon jug, and wrapped it in old burlap feed sacks soaked in cold water.

When the raking started, this was when I became part of the haying crew, and I thought that I was a man, and no longer had to only do "kid chores". I was about 6 or 7 when I was first put on the dump rake and drove the oldest, slowest and most steadfast team that we owned. I was shown how to step on the foot lever, and how to make long even windrows, and told to keep my elbows tucked in next to my body. When the tines would come up, there was a long metal lever that was for hand dumping that would fly past your elbow. If your arm was a little "too far out" it would hit your funny bone very hard. We used to say that raking hay taught you good table manners, to keep your elbows down, tight to your body and off the table. It would only take a couple of these whacks.... you learned quickly.

I soon knew how to harness, and hook up horses.

The next step was to rake down these long windrows and put the hay in as big a piles as possible. My dad had made a Buck Pole 16 feet wide, out of 8x8 timbers, with a stand on it about 36 inches high to push the hay against. You hooked a team of horses on each side with a 12 foot chain, with a man driving each team standing on the 8x8 timber, and leaning against the 36 inch upright that was gathering up the hay piles. When you were pushing as much hay as the horses could reasonably pull you would head for the haystack. In front of the stack there was a ramp on skids. It was ten feet tall and was a 45 degree angle up, with a stop on each side. When you got to the ramp, the teams would go out to each side of the stack. The horses knew that it was a hard pull and that they had to give a little extra. If you stalled half way up you had a mess that would have to be forked out by hand. When you got to the stop on the top, the teams had to be stopped immediately, or the hay and buck pole would end up on top of the man building the stack. The horses turned around and they then pulled the buck pole down, and away you went for another bunch of hay. The horses got very used to having to pull hard going up the ramp. Many times they would rear and plunge in anticipation of the hard short pull, and quick stop.

I was a lot older before I was allowed to do this job, but after doing it for years always felt that this was how I learned to be a good teamster. The horses seemed to know if you had good hands, and you could tell them, through how you handled the lines, what to do without saying a word. This method of stacking was very sloppy, and there was always a lot of re-raking to do behind the buck pole.

The quietest team was still on the hay rake, and dad had hired a little old man for that job, for I was now a teamster. This man was so funny, and enjoyed raking. He always smoked a little corncob pipe. He would stop and light his pipe, and say, "you know these horses are so well trained that they stop every now and then just to see if I haven't said Whoa and they had missed it". I don't know why he never set the meadow on fire with all that dry hay, but it never happened.

From haying you went to cutting your grain with the binder, stooking, and then thrashing. I was in charge of my first thrashing outfit when I was 15 years old. I hated it because I always had to be out early in the morning to be all greased up and ready to go by the time the first men arrived, and had to stay late to fix, and shut down the outfit.

One dangerous job was hauling green feed bundles down our high hill into the yard. The horses braced back against the breaching harness, but were not strong enough to hold the heavy load. As I reached the brow of the hill, I would jump down and place a long pole through the spokes of both back wheels of the wagon. As you went forward it would lodge on the reach of the wagon, and stop the wheels from turning, as you had no brakes. You then skidded to the bottom of the hill, stopped, backed up the team a step, pulled out the pole, and were on your way again. This was my invention of brakes.

The straw stacks in the fields had to be fenced before you could turn your cows out into the stubble fields. If you did not, the cows would eat around the bottom, and the stack soon looked like a gigantic mushroom. Many people lost quite a few cows by the smothering effect, when the tons of straw fell, and covered them as it caved in.

We had an old hip roof barn that had once been a house. My Dad had moved it in with teams of horses on wagons. We used the upstairs for a hayloft, and filled it as full as possible for the milk cows, and the workhorses. I don't know why it didn't burn down as we always used a lit kerosene lantern for light in the loft. We'd light up the lantern, hook it over our arm, and climb up the ladder into the loft. We would then hang it over a nail, and fork hay down into the mangers. Imagine a kid walking over dry hay with a lighted kerosene lantern!

With not much shelter for the animals we would make sheds by cutting small trees and nail them upright about two inches apart, and make two walls two and a half feet apart. Between these walls we put straw, and tramped it down. We would end up by putting poles on the roof, and covered it with straw. It had partitions, or stalls made in the same manner. You could house your pigs, chickens, calves etc. all in the same shed. When the temperature dropped these sheds would frost up and become very warm and comfortable inside. If it was a long cold winter, and your feed ran short, many times you would feed the barn to the cows come spring just to keep them alive. The homesteader's sense of humor said, "It is better than feeding them snowballs."

When the heavy winter snow came you would lift the hayrack off the high-wheeled wagon and put it onto the bob sleigh. Then hauling winterfeed would begin in earnest. We had to haul hay two miles from the meadow, and it was a job that went on all winter. After you got a trail made in the snow the horses would follow it, and you could run behind and keep warm. Our hayrack had two sleepers sticking out behind it a couple feet. If you got tired running, you could jump on and ride for a while to catch your breath. God help you if you fell down, because the horses were usually on the fast trot because they knew that there was feed, and a warm stall waiting at home.

As the winter wore on, the trail would build up with each new snowfall, sometimes reaching two or three feet deep. When spring came, and it warmed up, the snow would get rotten. The horses would stumble on the trail, and slip off, or the sleigh would slide off the edge, and tip over. All you could do was unload your hay out of the rack. You would then grunt, and curse to get the rack upright again and back on the sleigh. Next you had to swing the team and sleigh around through the deep snow, and fork on your whole load of hay again. This could happen several times on one trip.

The worst winter that I can remember was when there was so much snow that the stacks were half covered with snowdrifts. First you had to shovel snow down from the eight-foot high haystack, and then drive as close as you dared, and not get your team stuck in the drift. Next you would fork the hay from the stack onto the snowbank, then you had to go over and pitch the hay from the pile you had just made onto the hayrack. After you had your load of hay loaded, you would be wringing wet with sweat, to start the two mile journey home. This routine repeated itself all winter, but despite the hardship, people still seemed to have more time for fun than they do now.

It always seemed that I was constantly using forks. The bundle fork was a three tined fork, designed specifically to pick up the bundles. The big 5 tine straw fork enabled you to lift large amounts of loose straw. The hayfork had tines that were close together and very short to enable you to dig into the compact haystacks. The manure fork had 5 tines closer together for obvious reasons. The last fork was the potatofork, used to dig out our potato crop. We then had to haul these 5 gallon buckets down into the dirt cellar, to dump them into the big potato bin. This was our winter food supply, plus seed for the next year as well. One had to be careful not to break the handles on these forks, as they were expensive to replace.

Sauerkraut was made in 5 or 8 gallon crocks and stored downstairs with the rest of the vegetables so it would not freeze.

Another job you had to do was gather wood. Many of the Pioneers had some trees on their land but choose to steal wood off section 39. Knowing that there are only 36 sections in a township you can appreciate the saying!

Usually these people would go onto Government land and swipe the wood to save their own trees. Sometimes on a nice day you and some of your neighbors would meet to socialize and cut wood.

The main driving force was human muscle, swinging the axes. No one ever hauled wood or logs in the summer as the wooden wheeled wagons were to rough and heavy to pull with the horses. The sap was running in the trees in the summer and they were much heavier and harder to dry out to be able to burn them in your stoves. Using a sleigh you could pile on a mighty load of logs, but had to be very careful going down the hills. Sometimes the team of horses couldn't hold back the heavy load, so you had some wild sleigh rides.

On the prairies we didn't have big trees, only four or five inches across at the bottom end. Dry wood was a real prize, as it burned better, and gave off more heat. If you could find dead trees they weren't nearly as heavy to lift. With the axe you had to learn to cut the tree properly, so it would fall where you wanted it, or it would hang up in a standing tree. You then had to cut off the limbs and drag the tree out to the sleigh. You lifted the heavy end over the front sleigh bolster, and the smaller end over the back bolster. Most bobsleds had bolsters on them built for hayracks, sticking up about 18 inches. I always cut extensions about four feet high, so I could pile the trees on as high as I could lift. Most trees were limbed off at about 14 feet, so that they would not drag on the ground. I could usually cut a load of wood in about four or five hours of steady chopping and loading.

One nice warm day I had driven two miles with the team and sleigh and went to work. I had a nice big load, and jumped on and was ready to head for home. I was dead tired and ready for a smooth ride home. I clucked to the team to go. They tried but couldn't budge the load. The sleigh runners had gotten warm on the way there, and after sitting that long while I was loading, they had frozen to the ground.

What do you do?? You unload most of your load, take a log and pry the four runners loose, then swing the horses left and right on the pole and pull ahead. You then drag the trees forward and reload. Needless to say when I got home very late that afternoon I was about hungry enough to start chewing on those logs.

When you had many loads stockpiled you would have a wood-sawing bee with someone who had a buzz saw that ran off a drive pulley belt on a tractor. The buzz saw blade was 36 inches in diameter and two men would lift the logs up, and another would push the log into the spinning blade. The last man would take the cut off piece and toss it onto the big woodpile. Many mitts and fingers were sawed off, along with the trees in those days.

The wood would be cut and thrown to make a big woodpile. Then all you had to do was spilt it and haul it into the house as needed. This was very modern at the time, but if you lived far away from someone with a buzz saw, you would spend the best part of that winter on the working end of a bucksaw cutting your own wood.

I remember one time my Grandfather saying how tired he got of sawing wood, so he just left the heater door open, and kept pushing the log into the fire as it burned. When he had first arrived in this country he built a sod house on his quarter section in the middle of nowhere. It was much warmer than a wooden house, but hard to keep clean, plus the mice loved to move into the warmth of it during the winter. Many times I remember Grandma saying how they would collect as many buffalo chips as possible in the summer to see them through the hard winter, in case they ran out of wood.

During the winter my Grandfather would ski to Hardisty, 45 miles away for supplies, mainly salt, sugar, and flour. He would carry these home on his back, up to 150 pounds at a time. One story was told to me of Grandfather coming home with his heavy load. It was getting dark and he was very tired. He stopped at someone's straw stack, and buried himself there until morning. He was just getting settled in for a sleep, and there was a rustle in the stack. He said "Oh excuse me I didn't mean to bother you". The next morning he realized that he had made a bed beside two big sow pigs. Many of the pioneers did this all year to survive, and to get their mail. They had to drive oxen to break the land but they moved too slowly to go any distance. To my generation it seemed like a very tough life with an endless amount of work. I can certainly appreciate what they had to go through.

Chimney fires where always a constant threat. They were often the end-result of creosote forming from the sap in the wood, building up in the stovepipes. Many times I remember my mother throwing salt on the fire in the stove that had flared up. This would extinguish the hot fire, and let the stovepipes cool down, so the house would not catch on fire. There were no such things as fire extinguishers, or fire regulations in those days. It was a dirty filthy job to pull the stovepipes apart and take them outside where you would bang out the soot with a stick. This had to be done at least once a year.

When burning green poplar wood creosote would form in the pipes, and sometimes the black sticky liquid would drip down he walls. I can remember the pleasant smell of creosote, especially on a still clear winter day. It would drift for miles, along with the smell of wood smoke.

The house where I was brought up was very small compared to today's standard, but could be heated reasonably well with a wood cook stove and a heater. Using coal to heat with was considered a luxury that no one could afford. At night you would jam in the biggest log that would fit into the heater, and hoped that it would last until morning. Nine times out of ten, or if it were very green, it would smolder or not burn at all. Needless to say by morning there was frost on your blanket, and it was very cold. If you slept too close to the wall your hair would even freeze to the boards. We had never heard of pjamas in those days, and always slept in our fleece lined or long wooly underwear, with the one button trap door.

We didn't have indoor plumbing. In the morning when nature called we would just jam our feet into the cold felt boots, and head for the outhouse. By the end of March the snow would build up on the path and it was like walking down a hen roost. Many times you would slip off into the deep snow, and get your boots full of snow, With freezing hands and feet you would sit by the old cook stove shivering while mother or dad were trying to coax a fire to burn from the small kindling out of the old wood box, which always sat beside the stove. This wood box was never too fancy but was a major piece of furniture, and sometimes had to serve as a chair. It was an unwritten law that when you walked by the woodpile you would always bring an armload of wood and dump it in the wood box.

The Pioneers tried to split and dry the wood but sometimes in the cold of winter the wood was frozen with all the sap, and moisture in it. It did not dry until you brought it into the warm house to thaw out. My Grandfather used to do double duty by putting some blocks of wood on the oven door of the old cook stove. He would sit on top of the logs, wearing his tall felt socks and bib overalls, and smoke his stubby crooked little pipe. He didn't speak good English, or ever speak of his past. The look of contentment on his face by just being warm, showed the memories of past had been forgotten.

Now it certainly amuses me to see a young father in a camp sight swinging an ax and splitting logs to impress his family about his ability as a provider.

All man and beast would welcome spring. Man shed his winter underwear, and the beasts shed their heavy winter hair. The call of the Canada Goose flying north in a "V" was a sure sign that spring was coming, and that we had all survived another prairie winter.

As a kid we did not have much land to work, but on the other hand, our machinery was so old, and so small that I swear some of it had Roman Numerals on it. My Grandfather brought the original grain seed from the United States when he came up to homestead. He broke his soil with a team of oxen and the walking plough. Ten inches of soil was turned every trip down a row. An acre is half a mile long by 16 feet wide. You can imagine how many trips this took to prove up your homestead, and break up the designated 40 acres. If you hit a rock your plough would bounce out of the furrow, and could damage man or machine. You would then have to pull it back, and start again where it came out of the ground. Grandfather also told of how when you worked oxen, that you had to do your work very early in the morning, and late in the evening. During the heat of the day the flies and mosquitoes would drive the oxen half crazy, and they would run into the nearest slough, and just stand there, and could not be driven out. Some pioneers drove their oxen with lines, and bits in their mouths, while others simply commanded Gee and Haw (right and left), using a whip to train them.

After the sod was turned you had to harrow it to get it smooth. Later on some people would hook up to ten diamond tooth harrows in a row on a wooden draw bar pulled by the horses. The farmer then pulled a two-wheeled cart behind this so he could ride, and not have to walk behind in the dust like the earlier settlers. They would broadcast the seed by hand, and then reharrow it again until the grain kernels were covered. When they sprouted the roots would grow into the soft ground where there were nutrients and moisture.

When the ground was packed well the crop would come up much more evenly. You then waited for the crop to germinate, and the rain to come and keep it growing well. If you had frost on your grain the previous fall it would germinate poorly or not at all.

Most farmers would count out 100 kernels of grain and then put them in rows of five, and twenty down in a moist woolen sock. You then rolled up the sock, and put it in a quart jar with a lid on to keep it moist and warm. In the early years when the house would be freezing at night many a homesteader would take his jar of seed to bed with him to keep it warm. You waited at least ten days, and then you would take out the sock and count the kernels that had sprouted to get your percentage germination. You needed at least 85% germination.

The next step was to put the grain through the old hand Fanning Mill. This took out the weeds and the chaff, so that the clean grain would go through your drill evenly.

My dad used to sharpen his own plowshares and also do many neighbors. He loved to blacksmith and had a blower and a forge. I can still remember him lifting the shares out of the hot coals. They would be red hot and sparkling. He would then lay them on the Anvil and pound them into a sharp edge, so they would dig into the ground, They needed to have just the right angle, so that they would not just dig into the ground, or come out of the ground.

When cultivated acres were small the family would go out and walk through the crop to pull out the weeds, and the wild oat plants. Soon new weeds and diseases started to come to our area. Many of these spores were carried in by the winds blowing from the south and the east. Smut, rust and ergot, plus insects descended on the prairies. We had our share, but were never bothered by sawflies, which could chew into the green stems, and the plants would fall over and die. When you had rust or smut the harvesting machines would be red or black., and the kernels of grain would look like small mouse turds.

There were no tractor cabs in those days, so at night when you had to blow your nose it was all black or red. Imagine what it was doing to your lungs!

Ergot was terrible as it would form on wheat like a big growth, and if the animals ate it they were likely to loose a limb or two, ears, and or tails. My father tried many different remedies to combat diseases in his grain. For smut he would mix up formaldehyde with water, and pour it over a wagon box filled with seed wheat, and let it drain out. The old wagon box was pretty porous and the solution would leak out onto the ground, where the old laying hens would drink it. I guess that it must have been like kool aide for them because none of them died, and they kept on laying eggs.

Some weed seeds can stay in the soil for 25 years, and remain dormant. When growing conditions were right they would all grow! Wild oats was a prime example. We had one quarter section that had been hay land for at least 10 years, and when it was cultivated, within one month it was solid red root pigweed. Where the seeds came from I don't know.

In our part of the prairies you had to work up your tame grassland every so often, as the grass would get old and tired, and your yields would be very small. We would make hay off these lands for about five years, then graze it for about the same length of time, before it was time to cultivate it up and reseed it again the following year. With no weed sprays available you had to depend on the best agricultural practices available, and hope for the best.

The native Prairie Wool you just looked after very carefully and never overgrazed it or it would take years to recover. You also had to worry about prairie fires, and stubble fires. We had no country fire departments in those days and you and your neighbors fought fire by hand with wet gunnysacks and shovels.

During the summer or growing season there was very little time for rest. However most people made time for picnics, and country dances. Weeds, insects, animals, mother nature and the governments were always on our minds.

Insects could be brutal. Sometimes they would just move in and devour everything that was green. As kids we had to go out and pick off the potato bugs and squash them either by stepping on them or using two stones. There never was so many of them that the pick and squish method didn't work pretty well.

Grasshoppers could be like a plague and could wipe out an entire crop very quickly. Some farmers tried mixing arsenic with sawdust and walking around the boundaries of their fields, spreading it out with a spoon or a stick. One neighbor had a disaster with this. He didn't get the poison all spread and one day his cows somehow got into the mixture, and ate it. The cows all died, and the calves being thirsty nursed the dead cows and they died as well, as the poison had spread to the milk. Nowadays there is a spray for most insects, but if conditions are right they can still move in and devour a crop very quickly. This is the reason that you must check your crops very often, and regularly.

Most farmers and ranchers know that it is a way of life that you must compete with nature, but still we haven't found an antidote for governmental interference. There had been a strychnine poison out of years, but thanks to some smart person in government, it was taken off the market. Gophers come above ground three times a summer, and so no matter how hard you tried, you could never get them all. They did so much damage. People would say to me.

"Why don't you just shoot them?"

For four years running I would buy a case of 22 shells which amounted to 4,000 shells a year. I would drive out on my quad in the morning and evening and just shoot. I was a pretty good shot and had about a 90% kill rate. One evening when the sun was shinning I drove out to a canola field and looked through my riflescope. All I could see were those little devils eating the small canola seedlings! When a canola seedling is chewed off it never comes back. They reminded me of those thousands of little pac- men you used to see on your D.V.D.'s.

That summer I was at a Cattle Growers Meeting in Calgary. The ranchers from the eastern slopes were whining to try to get a bounty paid for the bear, and the wolves. If they found a dead year-ling worth about $600, and they didn't even know what the animal had died from for sure, but they wanted to be paid by the govern-ment. That same year the gophers had stripped over 90 acres of our canola and I don't know how much cereal crops. I guessed that they cost us $30,000 that summer. Compare that to one dead yearling worth $600!

There were no chicken or turkey hatcheries in those days so you had to keep a rooster and a turkey gobbler around to do their job. Turkeys were so stupid, as they would lay eggs all over the farmstead, and you would have to find the eggs and keep them warm until the hen finally decided to set. If an old chicken hen decided to get broody first, she would usually get the eggs to hatch. It took 28 days. The same routine was for a clucky hen, who would sit on 15 eggs for 21 days to incubate them. Eggs were a very important part of your farming, as you could sell them for grocery money. The clucky hen would stop laying eggs. If you had too many of them you did not get enough eggs to eat. The usual method to solve that was to dunk the hen into ice-cold water. After a couple of these treatments, she would forget about being broody, and start laying eggs again.

We always had a big garden, and of course milked cows, so we could have lots of fresh milk to drink and cream to separate. We made our own butter, and shipped a couple five gallon cans of cream each week to the creamery. The money from all this hard work was used for the remaining groceries that we had to buy, and any other bare necessities that we needed.

As kids we were never bored and as I always say when you are raised on junk and learn to fix things, it is sometimes better than having everything new. Just like lying to a banker supposedly builds character.

I'm not sure that I am a character, but I have told a lot of stories to bankers over the years just to keep my farm going.

Grandfather Kemper Breaking the sod

Old Wagon & Cousin Bob driving Niger & Jerry

Chapter 6
Rosie

When you think of our Old West, most often you just think of the men who made our history. However in our part of the world amongst the earlier settlers we had some very colorful or eccentric ladies (If I may use the word loosely)

One such lady ran two hotels, one with a beer parlor. According to the liquor laws of the day, a woman could not enter the beer parlor of the establishment, or the hotel would loose their liquor license. Therefore Rosie would sneak around on the second floor above the bar, to listen in to the men as they drank their beer, smoked, chewed snuff, spat and told stories.

It was very dark in these old buildings, with no electricity. The heat from the old pot bellied stove would rise up through the grate in the ceiling to heat the top story. One late night as Rosie was about to eavesdrop on the bar, one of her long skinny legs slipped down through the heat register and was dangling through the ceiling in the middle of the bar room full of men.

Before she could get herself braced to pull it back up, some quick thinking fellow jumped up on the table and grabbed her by the ankle, and held her there. I was told that they slapped it, tickled it and finally got an old pen, and scribbled some indecencies on her before letting her go. When she got loose she came down stairs into the bar ready to do battle. All the men were quietly sitting talking about ranching and farming. She was ranting and raving and promising to kill everyone in the room, plus some of their newborn.

Finally one young fellow drawls out, "what's the matter Rosie…. couldn't you sleep? Are you having a bad night?"

Another adds "You shouldn't be in here you could loose your license you know".

Again she called them all down and left the bar, in a killing rage, painfully limping upstairs.

Now Rosie did have a husband but after the hotels were built he disappeared. Some people thought that he was still standing in the cement….. supporting the west wall.

Rosie did have a lot of very fancy clothes and hats. Something like a fine Kentucky lady would wear on a Sunday afternoon walk with the family. Each year on fair days in Provost Rosie would pack several suitcases full of cloths, and catch the morning train to go there. She would go to her hotel in Provost, change into her vaudeville type cloths, walk out to the fair grounds and parade up and down in front of the grand stand and through the exhibits, twirling her parasol. She would return to the hotel, change into a different oufit, and go through the same performance sometimes five or six times a day, then return home on the midnight train to Cadogan. She would do this as long as the fair was on, sometimes several days in a row.

Rosie had an old buggy and an old standard bred horse that had both seen better days. The harness needed polish, the buggy paint, and the old standard bred horse tried his best to look stately, as she drove down the main street, but he was just too old and tired. The town kids would sometimes run along beside, and tease her, but they never got too close as Rosie had a long Bamboo buggy whip with a little leather lash on the end. She could take a horse fly off the ear of her horse and never touch the horse. Many "smart alec" kids got too close and felt the end of the whip on their ear, or neck.

Rosie was indeed a sight when she drove into town for groceries. All dressed up in her Vaudeville type fancy cloths, complete with men's work boots, and woolen socks. She always wore a big hat and bright red lipstick. One day she drove in and just sat in front of the store. Finally the storekeeper came out and asked if she was having trouble. "Yes" she said in a very ladylike tone. "When I sat on the buggy seat it went down and when I try to get up it has me pinched. Will you please jump up and put some weight on the boards so I can get free?" The poor fellow didn't know what to do, so just stood there looking at her. Finally Rosie roared out.

"Don't just stand there like the village idiot get up here and put your weight on the buggy seat so I can get free".

When Rosie bought groceries she always had the time, day and year written on the top of her bill. I guess that this was her way of book keeping, as she would go home and write it on her calendar, so she would know what time of year it was.

Rosie had a very ingenious way of getting her meat too. Small amounts of grain was sprinkled on the ground outside her window. She made a trap out of an old bed spring propped up by a stick with a string tied to it and ran the string up into her window. She would sit at her kitchen window and watch. When the prairie chickens and partridge came to feed she would pull the string, bringing down the bedspring on top of the birds, killing or trapping them.

On one such occasion during a very cold day a young man from town came out to cut wood for her. He knew that Rosie didn't keep a very clean house so tried to avoid mealtime. However this day Rosie said that she was roasting a fresh partridge, and that it was so cold that he must stay and eat.

Reluctantly he agreed, but he nearly fainted when she opened the oven door. There was the bird roasting nicely, and right beside it in the oven was the chamber pot being thawed out.

I don't know how dinner went but he lived to a ripe old age, so I guess it didn't hurt him. He still continued to chop her wood, but always made sure that he was never there anytime near meal-time I don't know what ever happened to Rosie or where she was even buried, but she was definitely a colorful character in our old early west.

Sleigh

CHAPTER 7

MOONSHINE

Moonshine, Home Brew, White Lightning, or anything that would ferment, played an important role in our early western history. In the late 1800's and past the turn of the century when the first North West Mounted Police came west their most important job was to try to control moonshiners and whiskey traders bringing their product across the border.

It kept them busy full-time as there was a steady flow, both ways across the 49th parallel. Horse and Cattle Rustling wasn't even a close second in the list of crimes of the time to solve. The Whiskey Traders had very few morals. They would trade their product to the Indians for furs, horses, or anything of value. They were only interested in the quantity they could trade, not the quality. They would cut the stuff with kerosene, lye, and God knows what else to increase the volume and make it potent. The Indians would get high on this firewater and begin to pass out, or fight and kill each other. Those who got a tomahawk between the ears and were killed were sometimes the lucky ones. Others died in pure agony, as this cocktail would eat their throats, and intestines. This would cause a very long and painful death.

There were many means of disguising the transport of the brew, which was made of anything that would ferment. One of the most unique was a young fellow dressed as a traveling minister, selling Bibles. There was a big run on Bible Sales. The R.C.M.P. became suspicious because there weren't that many people that could read, or write, let a lone spend time reading the Holy Book. A police officer went out and purchased a Bible. Low and behold the pages had been carved out to hold a container of whiskey.

An oilman once told me about putting in a pipeline along the U.S. Border in southern Alberta and Saskatchewan. Even a hundred years later it was not uncommon for your caterpillar tractor to drop into an invisible hole. They often found the remains of the old whiskey still, and equipment still intact.

The early pioneers made some very good moonshine, and they always liked to treat their fellow neighbors to a drink when they came to visit. Of course they didn't want the police snooping around, and they were also very reluctant to report any known moonshiner, because of fear of retaliation. For example getting your hay burned, or finding your best milk cow shot.

Some early brewers just made wine, while others took it further and distilled the product, and had the mash as a left over.

There were many uses for the mash. One of our neighbors claims that he used to soak wheat in whiskey and feed it to the prairie chickens. They would get so drunk that they couldn't fly, so he could just go out and whack them on the head with a stick, and had fresh meat, any time of the year.

Now in those days hardly anybody could afford whiskey so I'm sure that he had just fed them the mash.

One of our relatives ran an experimental farm on the prairies. The Government tested all kinds of methods of making cattle feed. They were the first in the area to have a wooden tower silo to store cattle feed. When the feed fermented the juice would seep through the cracks. It never froze even in the coldest weather. The sparrows would fly down and sip this juice, and pretty soon could not get airborne again. Along would come the old barn cats, which would catch a few of these intoxicated birds. No one knew whether or not the alcohol got through to the cats, but they would stretch out on the sunny side of the barn and sleep all afternoon and have a peaceful catnap.

We had one old bachelor in our area that always came to visit us with his little team of dappled grays hooked to his one seat buggy.

When he came it was usually a two-meal stay, and he never would leave until at least midnight. He always liked me when I was a little boy. I was a good friend to him out on the big prairies and would always help him unhook, stable, and feed his team. Now I won't say that Harry was a little slow but he was the kind of guy that might pee on an electric fence. He always had a saying when surprised that came out as "Ma Gracious"! He would never hurt a fly, but someone had reported that he was making moonshine. When the police arrived with a search warrant he just said "Ma Gracious Come On In, and do your search, all I have is a couple of quart sealers of vinegar. "I make my own vinegar to process my pickles, and buying vinegar is very expensive you know". The Mounties couldn't find any vats, or bubbling crocks, but these two jerks confiscated his two big Mason Jars of vinegar. The only problem was that upon analyses the vinegar tested 23% alcohol, so poor old Harry had to go to court. The judge said,

"Mr. Sommers would you please approach the bench. You know that you have broken the law so I must fine you $45 dollars, and from now on would you please buy your vinegar."

The judge then gave him a sly wink and said "I'll bet those pickles were good."

This was not all Mr. Sommers bad luck, a year later his house burned down, and 5,000 bedbugs were left homeless and unemployed.

About that same time, a little further down the road, there lived a couple who made moonshine in 45 gallon wooden barrels. I think that they must have sold a lot of it, because the horse and buggy traffic down their road was quite heavy and I don't think that any family could drink that amount.

Some how the police got wind of the enterprise, so sent out a young inexperienced corporal to investigate. The husband saw the mountie coming riding up the road. The R.C.M.P. knocked on the door and presented the search warrant, declaring that he had orders to search the place.

The husband stated that he certainly didn't mind the search, "but can you wait a little while, as my wife is having a bath in the other room."

It was a two-room shack. She had actually jumped into the moonshine barrel and was making a lot of splashing noises.

The young mountie was quite embarrassed, and said. "I will come back a little later in the day," and retreated. He came back later, and found nothing.

I don't know to this day what they did with that batch, but I'll bet that one barrel of moonshine had a distinct flavor, and a little extra kick.

There was the odd good side benefit to home brew. It helped many a shy young man get up the nerve to ask a neighbor girl out on a date. Now these weren't bad boys. They could handle the meanest cow, or fork the wildest bronc, but to ask a pretty young girl for a dance, and a date took about 3 or 4 shots of white lightening. She would know and understand. When it came time for the big date he would be the perfect gentleman. Many of these outings ended up in marriage and a lifelong commitment to each other.

The next story came from a friend of mine but I have no reason to doubt this escapade, as his Dad was one of the leading characters.

The thrashing machine had shut down because of rain. The threshing crew had not been to town for a long time, and they felt that it was time for a little fun. Ole was a big tall Norwegian who swore that Leif The Lucky had discovered Canada because he was the Bravest of the Brave. Ole was such a quiet man that if he didn't have a drink or two in him, you would almost need a pry bar to get a word out of him. Chaude was of Scottish dissent, a big happy man with reddish hair, who never started a fight, but could sure finish one! The smile never left his face whether he was winning or l oosing. Tommy was a little short Englishman, about 5 feet 4 in stature. It was said that, "you can always tell an Englishman, but you couldn't tell him much". He had a huge handle bar mustache, and a nose that looked as if it had had been rearranged. He had the temperament of a one eyed tom cat, and used to beat his family regularly. When he carried the feed to the pigs, he was so short that the buckets would drag on the snow.

Ole had a little Chevy coupe with two doors and a small back window for the back seat. The three piled into the car and off to town they went to get rowdy. It was a long way to Czar, in those days the roads were very poor and bumpy. After the first three miles they decided they were thirsty so stopped at the old moonshiners place and bought a gallon jug of his best brew. Some people claimed that you could pour a bit of this on a spoon, and when you held a match to it that it would burn a bright blue flame.

They closed down the bar in Czar and headed home very late at night. Tommy was in the back seat. With all the bumpy roads, he announced in his fine English Accent,

"I believe that I am about to be ill"

Claude responded, "Roll down the back window, and stick your head out. I don't want you throwing up in this car."

Ole had the Chevy wide-open going down Tommy's driveway lined with tall bright sunflowers. He had it right to the mat and was going all of thirty miles an hour, weaving through the Sunflowers. When they arrived at Tommy's house Claude said "get out Tom."

There was no response. He was either passed out from the brew, or knocked out from all the big sunflower heads hitting him, as he threw up. Claude reached between the two seats, grabbed Tommy by the belt and pulled him out of the car like you would pull a rubber plunger out of the toilet. Ole got out, grabbed Tommy's tweed cap, and wiped the puke off his dear little Chevy coupe. They picked up Tommy by the armpits, and threw him into his house, and headed for the bunk house.

The next morning they were up bright and early ready to go threshing. No Tommy! His wife met them as they approached the step. "What have you done to my man?"

They said nothing but took a quick peek in the door. There was Tommy still in the entry, sound asleep, all bruises, and his nose rear-ranged again.

Weather we approve or disapprove, alcohol was a part of our heritage. It could have the tendency to lower social inhibitions, but it also had medicinal purposes for both man and animal. We always kept a flask of whiskey in the tack room and saddlebag. About 4 or 5 ounces of whiskey was the best known cure for a half frozen baby calf. One hired man felt that this was a big waste of good whiskey. One night in the middle of a blizzard we made an agreement. He could drink his 3 ounces, but then had to give the freezing slimy calf mouth-to-mouth resuscitation. The calf lived, and the man was happy. So all ended well.

CHAPTER 8
BARN DOOR INFLUENCE

Some of you were brought up in very loving and Christian home. I was not so let's just say that you might have a head start on me to get through the pearly gates. We had no religion in our home, and very little affection. I had good parents and as much food as a boy could want.

We all have our own ideas of what our God is like. We even may feel that sometimes we know what he looks like. Well mine has ridden with me many miles, and is a happy and good-natured guy. We have been through many things in my lifetime and I'll bet that there are many times that he has just looked down and shook his head and said,

"If I can just keep that cowboy between the white lines he will someday come and knock on my door".

For some reason I always seemed to believe that there was a God and a Heaven.

It seemed very strange to me that everybody had to attend church for weddings and funerals, but would never go on Sundays. When their children would marry or someone would die they wanted the full nine-yard function with all the stops pulled out on the organ at the church.

We had one family in our District that went to church every Sunday... You would call them very frugal. In their minds they were good Christians, and who are we to say that they weren't. It was a riot.

They used to have silver collection plates at the church. When the eldest boy would pass the plate over his Mother to his Dad, he would hold one hand over the top of the plate as if to be depositing his offering, and flip up his thumb to snap the bottom of the plate, so it would sound like coins hitting the plate.

I came from a very small town in east Central Alberta. It is called Metiskow. It is an Indian name meaning Many Small Sticks or trees.

When I was a boy they used to have red-hot Revival Tent Meetings there. My cousin and I used to sneak over on Saturday nights, to listen and watch, from the safety of the nearby trees.

There were many confusing things going on in my mind, and heart about religion. These Tent Meetings with their "Fire and Brimstone" preachers would yell and scream and carry on. Sometimes they even got down on the ground, and rolled around. Thus the name Holy Rollers!

They would cry for the Lord and many would be publicly saved in this "big whoop tee do". It might be less than a week later that some of these "newly converted" where out on the biggest alcohol binge you could imagine.

This was even more confusing because many of these guys parents looked down on me because I did not attend church, with their kind.

I still had my own beliefs and I kind of lived by them. Riding out on a good morning and watching the calves buck and kick, or watching a bumper crop coming, I knew that somebody was looking out for me. I guess that is why my favorite hymn is "The Place Where I Worship is the Wide Open Spaces".

Now don't get the wrong idea about me. I was no angel, but on the other hand I did not have a drug or alcohol problem. I guess when you are young, and you swing a pretty wide loop it can scrape the angel wings and halo off a healthy young man pretty fast.

I still avoid "IN YOUR FACE" religious people if I can.

There are many different churches, and to hear the people talk their congregation is always the best, the right one, and the only one. I still believe that there is only one God for all, and I am not the one here to judge anyone.

I'd like to tell you about a fine example of this. When I was a very young lad there was a little country school north and west of us called Daisey. It was a dirt-poor area in the sand hills, and most families felt very lucky to just have food on the table. One of the families had eleven kids. There were twenty pupils in the one room school, and there was no money for any extras, especially at Christmas. The teacher's wage was poor, so she couldn't buy Christmas bags for each child.

Now this was wintertime remember and cold. Anyway a bunch of local people, mostly ranchers were gathered in the Czar Hotel Bar…

To warm up of course!

They got talking about the Daisey School putting on a pie Auction so the kids could have a Christmas. One drink led to another, and they all decided that the thing to do was go up north and attend this party.

Those Cowboys didn't have a lot of money either but amongst themselves they bid those pies up to the skies.

You know that was the best Christmas those poor kids ever had. There were presents, candy and oranges for everyone.

Now I don't believe that there was one Christian among them, but their hearts were pure and I'll bet God makes allowances for such people.

Getting back to me again. I was still kicking over the traces alot yet, but probably wasn't doing anything any other normal person at my age would not do.

At a 4-H Banquet I met this young lady,… Diane ….. and believe me I was a goner……….

We dated for seven years before she could hobble me.

You know you can't rush into these things…………

After that life was wonderful.

The minister at our wedding thought that I should have a spiritual overhaul, but I sidestepped that, as I was still unsure about religion.

We travelled a lot, worked hard and danced a lot. Many a night in the old Town Hall of Metiskow we would dance until morning. Then one day Diane says, "Let's take Dancing Lessons."

I said "Why I'm a good dancer?"

She said, "I know Honey but I am tired of running backwards"!

You know this wasn't all bad either. Many a time I would do a 7 step over the corral fence with an old mad cow right behind me.

God gave me a sense of humor.

I have always been known as a storyteller, love humor

… not exactly a liar, but have been known to stretch the truth a little. Now thanks to our writers group I have put pen to paper, and started to write some of it down.

An example is a little short story of a friend of mine and I coming home from Seattle. Dave and I had stopped for supper in a little country western looking restaurant. At one of the tables there was about eight senior couples quietly sitting having coffee. As we got up to leave and walked by their table, one of the ladies turns to her husband, I presume, and in a loud voice ..says;

"Don't you Love Me?"

I stopped mid stride…looked her right in the eye and said.

"Mame….. Love you, I don't even know you!"

There was a dead silence for a few seconds and then the whole table cracked up. I kept on walking.

See what a little humor does to people. All the way home Dave kept giving me the gears about hitting on little old ladies.

Now I'm not going to tell you that I was a real bad dude, and that all of a sudden one day, I became saved.. Well I wasn't… I worked hard. I played hard, and going to church in those days was not a priority to me.

When I am finished this story you will realize that I am an old rancher, and that if you roped a colt and dragged it into a catch pen, it would jump at the fence, fight you and be unhappy, until you could finally settle him down, by showing him kind words and the rewards there.

However, if you were to guide him in with a gentle touch here and a little push there he would be much easier to settle down.

Now that is sort of what Cowboy Church is trying to do to me.

I often think of my favorite old story of a farmer who wanted to teach his son a lesson in consequences, and what would happen if he did something wrong. Every time the boy did something wrong he had to go and pound a nail into the barn door. I guess the door was getting pretty well covered.

One day the boy said to his Dad that he wanted the Lord to forgive him for all the bad things he had done. So the father took the boy down to the barn door and they pulled out all the nails.

He said, "Son your sins are now forgiven"… The boy was so happy that all his sins were forgiven, but noticed holes where the nails had been.

"How can I get rid of the holes?, he cried.

The Dad replied, "Today you chose to confess your sins to God and he will forgive you and help you deal with the consequences. However, while we live here on this earth the deep holes are ours to bear, and we cannot close some of them completely this side of Heaven. Hopefully God will mend them someday for you."

Sometimes I am still in that catch pen, and still take the odd jump at the corral fence. But I know that I can bow my head down and accept the bit gladly and peacefully.

Chapter 9
Reading Nature

In these modern times of environmental technologists and meteorologists, one wonders how the poor pioneer, without any sophisticated knowledge, could possibly exist without being able to predict the weather. If the whole truth were known, the men of the land probably were just as accurate at "guessing the weather"- as the experts of today.

They learned early in life to read the signs of the weather from nature. Leaves turned over, excessive poplar fuzz falling; dogs or cats eating grass are all signs of forecoming rain. You will also see that the common anthill is built up high with a fresh dirt ring around the entrance.

Excessive coyote howling usually heralds in a change of weather. Our ranch was along a creek flat thirteen miles from the nearest town of Metiskow, and the railroad tracks. Normally we never heard the trains. Anytime that you could hear them we knew that there would be a change in the weather- for the worst. If the train sounded extremely loud-watch out! As the barometric pressure drops, air becomes less dense, thus sound travels better and more clearly.

Livestock usually is restless before a storm, you will see cattle and horses running and bucking, and putting on quite a show. One of the most eerie experiences happened one beautiful winter day. As we looked out the window there were our range cows half way up the high hill in a tight bunch, continuously, slowly circling. This went on for over an hour. By evening we were beginning one of the worst three-day blizzards on record. Flocks of snowbirds usually appear ahead of Artic disturbances--snow or drifting snow.

A ring around the Moon warns of an impending storm. The numbers of stars within the ring represent the number of intervening days before the storm hits. Our water pressure system on a 250-foot deep drilled well normally pumped crystal clear water, expect a day or two before a storm, when all of a sudden there would be small amounts of sand in the water.

It has long been believed that the appearance of two sundogs means cold weather. The higher they are in the sky, the colder it will be. A sundog on the left side of the sun indicates a warming trend.

The sighting of a mirage usually means warm mild weather and was always a welcome sign for those of us living on the prairies. This was great mirage country, especially in February and March. Sometimes we have seen whole towns, grain elevators and all to the east, which we believed to be the towns of Denzel or Primate Saskatchewan, over 60 miles from us. Often the Neutral Hills were literally thrown up to meet the sky. Mirages have also been sighted in an upside down position.

Before a warming trend, if you look into the distance at the poplar and willow bluffs, they will appear to be a much darker color than normal. They will remain this dark color throughout the warm spell.

Heavy hoar frosts were always recorded on the calendar. It was believed that in six months you could expect rain. Thus a winter with a great deal of hoar frost brought hopes of an abundant supply of rain for the coming summer. We tracked it over many years. It didn't always bring rain, but there would always be some sort of a weather disturbance pass through. Thunder in January is said to mean a great deal of moisture within the next six weeks. Lightning in April is said to mean a dry year.

Clouds are often a good barometer. We think of a "windy" sunset, meaning that the clouds above the horizon appear pink or red and the setting sun often resembles a big, red fiery ball.

A trademark of the west, the Chinook Arch is always a welcome sign in the middle of a long winter. Where we lived Chinooks, were not as warm and occurred much less frequently than south of the

Neutral hills. Chinooks could also be problematic if you are grazing livestock on open range. These are called Bob Tailed Chinooks. There is a sudden and dramatic rise in temperature, snow melts, followed immediately by just as sudden a drop in temperature again. This freezes an ice cover over the grass. This ice cuts the cows noses and mouths as they attempt to forage. It would also cut the horses fetlocks as they pawed for feed.

There is an old story about one of the hottest quickest Chinooks in history. A family had gone to town with their team and bobsled. By the time they had their groceries and were heading home it was so warm that the children in the back of the sleigh all had their jackets off. In fact it was so warm that the team on a fast gallop along with the front bob were on the snow, yet the back bob was in the mud, and the dog trailing behind was swimming.

Since man first settled our country he has been a great predictor of the severity of each impending winter. Indian and White man alike watched such things as the growth of moss, actions of the birds and animals, and the thickness of their winter coats. Signs of a long severe winter are muskrats building high houses, squirrels and other rodents storing larger food supplies than normal. When butchering an animal the spleen was carefully observed. If the organ had white spots this warned of an early and cold winter. An even shaped spleen foretold of an even, mild winter.

Granny's rheumatism, and any who have had old bone fractures can usually tell you when a storm is coming.

Mother Nature can be kind and caring. She can bring you good growing conditions, and lots of rain, and great weather for calving, and her wildlife friend's growth.

Mother Nature can also be ruthless and killing, creating droughts, and conditions that started prairie fires, that would burn for several hundred miles, wiping out everything in its path, including some of our pioneers.

Mother Nature can bring you bountiful crops. You can have done everything correctly, using all the newest technology and methods to boost yields, and your crops can look like a million dollars. Then suddenly she will turn her back on you and wipe you out with hail, or an early massive frost in a matter of minutes or hours. This gives you no income for that year, but still lots of expenses.

Having ranched all our lives we have been dependent on Mother Nature, and have tried to work with her as much as possible. She has given us some wonderful bountiful crops, but there have been times when we have suffered her wrath. The thing that you must remember is that Mother Nature is always in command, and has the final say.

Out to Pasture

Chapter 10
Jock

As was usual in most small prairie towns there was an older man who had a big old team of slow Clydesdales, that used to haul garbage, freight and do the rural mail routes. This team could pull tons of weight, but speed wasn't in their code of ethics. The owner who we will call Jock hardly ever got excited either. One of his jobs was to clean up the town hall after a social was held. Before Jock could start cleaning up he had to do the hard part first, and that was to empty all the half full glasses of liquor. Any half drinks left on the table were not poured into the slop pail, but poured back by Jock. If you peeked into the hall later, or the next day you might still find Jock sound asleep.

Now in a small town there is always somebody belly aching and complaining about something. In Jock's case they said that he was too slow with his big team, and that the cream cans that he picked up would be frozen before they got back to town, that the mail was late, and many other small nuisances.

It seemed that the people that had the biggest houses, and seemed the best off always chiseled him the most when a job had to be done. Jock always said, "They won't chisel their way into heaven …the prices are all the same for one way." Most did not appreciate the fact that the town would have been a big stinking mess if it were not for him, hauling the garbage away.

Jock heard about this horse trader that had just acquired a team of the very fast coal black geldings. He thought that he would slip out on Sunday morning and have a look at them. Well it just happened this fellow was leading the team across the road. Both blacks seemed very well mannered, and Jock was ready to deal right then and there, but the trader said,

"I never trade on Sundays. If you are interested come back tomorrow."

Jock went home and dreamt that night of driving the new team, and getting the mail out on time, and of the cream cans not getting frozen.

The horse deal was done the next day, and a little boot, (or cash) was exchanged plus Jocks team of Clydesdales. The cash came out of Jock's old worn jeans.

The team of blacks seemed so well mannered, but after being tied in the barn and the nerve lines taken off, they were untamed, mean, and just plain spoiled horses. When Jock went to pull up the belly-band on the one it exploded. He thought that it was just the new surroundings, and that the horse would soon get over it. The next horse seemed better, but when the britching came down over his rump he started to kick, and every two minutes he would lash out with both hind feet.

Jock now started to think, and after a big mouthful of snuff, went over to the coffee shop to see if he could get some help to get hooked up to his little bob sleigh. On the way he muttered, "Never trust a man who will not deal on Sunday, especially a horse trader."

Jock had always bragged, "If I can get a line on them I can drive them"

His two friends agreed to help him. The horse that was kicking never stopped, so the handler just threw his coat, on the horse's head. This acted as a blindfold, and the horse settled down. The other fellow was an old wild horseracing cowboy, so he jumped on the horse's neck, grabbed him and started chewing on his ear to calm him down. The problem there was that he had been in too many wild horse races and didn't have many teeth left, and pretty well just gummed it. The result wasn't exactly what was hoped for.

After about twenty minutes of this stampede exercise, Jock jumped into the sleigh and grabbed the lines and yelled,

"Cut em loose Boys."

The team hit their collars and ripped out of the yard gate like they had been shot out of a ten gauge shot gun. The offside horse that had been blind folded couldn't adapt his eyes quickly enough, so half way up the street they made a hard left and knocked out the post holding up the veranda on the old coffee shop. This caused the back bob to skid sideways and knocked several boards off Carlson's old biffy. Grampa Carlson couldn't see or hear very well. He was just coming out of the outhouse and pulling up his old bib over-alls, when he noticed that the boards were ripped off. He took one look and mumbled, "I got to get Ma to ease back on the cabbage and broccoli."

By then the team had clamped the bits in their teeth and were in a full tilt run away mode. But give Jock his dues he was doing the best that he could under the circumstances. He had on his new four-buckle cowboy overshoes, that gave him good traction and had his feet braced on the front dashboard of the sleigh box. He was pulling back on the lines with all his strength and yelling,

"Whoa. Whoa. You Black Son's of Bitches."

He knew that if he could get across the railroad tracks, and into the big meadow that the team could run until they played out. After about half an hour, his arms felt like they were stretched about six inches longer, and the horses were slowing down, so he just threw the lines at them and screamed,

"Run …Run some more you black devils."

He encouraged them to run now, and did figure eights, played fox and goose, and any running game that he could think off. The sleigh tracks in the snow looked like some crazy jig saw puzzle, but finally the horses gave Jock the lines, and he could steer and stop them. After a couple of stops and starts he drove back into town, and right up to the post office, gently pulled the lines and said "whoa". The black team stopped with the sweat dripping off them, and the white steamy foamy lather coating the black harness.

Jock said, "Now boys, throw in the mail bags and empty cream cans. He then clucked to his new team, and went proudly up Main Street, at a pretty fast trot, just a little faster than his old team of

Clydes, but he knew that would improve. Now that extra boot that he had given to the horse trader for this team didn't seem to hurt so much.

He proudly wore his new 4 buckle overshoes, driving his new team of blacks, for the whole town to see.

Chapter 11
Old Cowboy Stories

There are so many stories and anecdotes of the cowboys that used to come from our area.

One took place at the small town rodeo of Czar, where the fences were rickety old poplar rails and some page wire that had probably been borrowed, or stolen, from the C.P.R. right of way fences.

One of the riders came out on a Brahma bull and lasted just long enough to get bucked off in the middle of the arena. He was kicked in the head and knocked unconscious, and there he lay in the middle of the arena. The bull circled the arena at a full trot shaking his horns, and daring anyone to challenge him. The pickup men didn't dare rope him because if they couldn't hold him he would crash the fence and maybe trample some of the crowd.

The funny part of it was that the ambulance, which also served as the local hearse was standing ready at the gate, but the undertaker would not bring it in, as it was brand new, and he didn't want to get a fender or some other part damaged by the mad bull.

After the bull had circled for about half an hour he finally found the out gate and ran out by himself. The crowd gave a sigh, and the undertaker opened the gate and drove up to the downed cowboy. By this time the cowboy had come to, and with the help of his friends walked out of the arena, and the stampede continued. No one had ever heard of concussion in those days.

Years later I was talking to that cowboy and asked him about the incident. He said, "Oh that was my fault as I was only half full of beer, and it sloshed to one side, and I couldn't get my balance back, and fell off."

At Dawson Creek a Cowboy friend of mine was about to nod his head to let his bull out, when the big Brahma hooked the chute gate with his horn, it came off the hinges and the bull tossed it on top of the gate man. The bull was bucking up and down on top of the chute gate, on the ground, on top of the chute man.

Everyone thought that he would be crushed, but luckily it had rained four inches the day before. The bull finally finished jumping on the gate and took off down the arena. Men rushed out and lifted up the gate. The pinned gateman scrambled up and ran for safety. In the mud there was a four-inch deep perfect imprint of the man.

The rider had bucked off, and said later that as he looked down when the bull was bucking on the chute gate he saw a pair of eyes staring back up at him through the planks. That had broken his concentration. He had ridden that bull four times previously, but there was no payday for the cowboy that day.

Another time that same cowboy and a couple of others were coming through Hobema, an Indian Reservation, in a Volkswagen, with their saddles and other gear strapped on top of it. The cowboys came upon a young Indian boy hitch hiking on the side of the road. They slowed down as if they where going to give him a ride. One of the cowboys had a starting pistol, which looked very real. They almost stopped, turned down the window aimed at the kid and shot a couple loud bangs. The Indian boy jumped the ditch, scrambled under the fence, and started running across the field flat out. He was out about 200 yards and they gave him a couple more shots.

The poor lad never did slow down even as he disappeared over the horizon.

Talk about playing Cowboy and Indians!

Another favorite story of mine is about our cousin. He and his parents fed the livestock and pulled the flags across the racetrack at the Calgary Stampede Chuck wagon races for many years. He didn't ever make it in the big times, but was voted Cowboy of the year in one of the smaller associations, and earned a trophy saddle.

One time after the Calgary Stampede was over he heard that they needed some cowboys over in Saskatoon. He loaded his family, of two little kids and his wife in their old car and headed east, to that rodeo. They didn't have money for a hotel room but his wife didn't mind because they parked by a golf course, and every time the sprinkler came on she could have a shower, with the kids. I guess that back home the only running water she ever had was when she broke into a fast trot from a walk, while carrying two pails of water from the well to the house.

One of our local Czar Ranchers decided to run chuck wagons at some of the small rodeos. He would unhook several of his working horses from the mowers, rakes, or whatever was handy, and hook the four fastest ones to the old chuck wagon, and the races were on. He was a great lineman and could turn those barrels like nobody I had ever seen.

At one rodeo he did the turn too sharp and tipped the wagon over and was knocked out cold. As he lay there unconscious his Dad ran out to him crying, "Don't just lie there like a big hairy bear…say something. And get up and look after your horses."

This Rancher came a long way in the sport of chuck wagon racing. The year he won Calgary he became eligible to compete in Cheyenne Wyoming. After the final race in Calgary he and his out-riders and crew were all having a big party at the Stampede grounds.

He returned from the pay window with a brown paper bag, which was full of his prize money. He tossed it on the ground and said, "Take what I owe you boys."

He had one big right lead horse called Yankee Storm. The horse was dark brown, with a coal black mane and tail. He bought him in B.C. and brought him home in the back of his old truck through a raging blizzard. Old Yankee had his head over the cab facing the storm and he never wanted to be passed. What a competitive spirit that horse had, and loved to run.

This expert teamster's quick turning onto the track was also the end for him because at the Cheyenne Rodeo he rolled his wagon and was killed. There was no money left so a local trucking company brought him, and his remaining horses home in the back of their cattle liner. Thus ended another chapter of old time rodeo. They gave it their all, and died broke but certainly gave the crowds many a thrill. He was such a big happy-go-lucky fellow who loved good times".

I had seen him in town just before he went to Cheyenne. He had said to me,

"Come along with me, I need a good strong cowboy. We'll show you a good time!"

Could you imagine, if I had gone? Me a young farm boy in Cheyenne at the biggest chuck wagon races in the United States, with no money and the boss man dead, trying to find a way to get home !

Floyd Scott on Shoney at Rumsey

CHAPTER 12
THE DIRTY THIRTIES

There were many sad stories that we heard from the era of the Great Depression, or "The Recession" as it was called. They were true and did not need exaggeration. There was no rain for years, but if you were lucky enough to get a crop, and had something to sell, it was not worth anything. My Uncle Louis shipped a load of market pigs to Edmonton. The next week in the mail he received a bill for the freight. The money that he was paid for the pigs did not cover the freight bill. He wrote the company and stated,

"I don't have any money, but I do have some more pigs."

Some of the dust storms lasted for days. It was so black that you could just make out the sun in a dirty gray haze. Imagine the poor farm wife trying to keep a fairly clean house without running water. Every door and window leaked in the fine dust. It got into every thing they owned, from the butter to the baby's diaper.

When the men came home in the evening after working in the dirt all day, it would be all over, in their ears, eyes and nostrils. They maybe had a small washbasin, and hand carried water to try to get clean. Not only did the pioneers have to live with the natural disasters and the dust storms, but they also had to get ready for another winter, and had bills to be paid. Back then there was no government subsidies, family allowances or any financial help at all. Many of them resorted to desperate measures. Many suicides occurred; while others burned their homes down to try to collect fire insurance. This may sound a little extreme, but until you have been there try not to judge them to harshly.

One family hid all their furniture in a haystack, and then set their house on fire. I remember this story in particular because the fellow was working on my uncle's threshing crew when the police came and arrested him. The insurance company had become suspicious and had shoved long rods through the stacks and found the furniture. The poor man cried like a baby when the police took him away.

At another farm north of my grandparents homestead, smoke was spotted. My Grandparents rushed to help. When they arrived, there was the lady of the house so nervous and scared that she was walking around the house still throwing lit matches at the house.

My Dad happened to be in town during the next story. The Post Master, who was in a wheelchair, claimed that he had been hit on the head and robbed, and then the robbers had set the place on fire.

My Dad wheeled out the poor man and saved his life.

Stories circulated that the robbers were seen some thirty miles away heading east in a Model T car. Later it was discovered that the Post Master had done the whole deed himself to cover up the fact that he had embezzled government funds from the Post Office.

The funny part of this story is that I had a similar experience, years later, in this same town. We were having a small town rodeo, and I was bringing in my metal corrals to use for the arena. It was about 6 o'clock in the morning, when Hans, a Swedish boy and I drove into town. There was an old two-story house with smoke billowing out of the windows. We rushed in calling out the names, as we knew who lived there. There was no answer. All the beds were made, and everything seemed in order. We couldn't find anyone.

We woke up the neighbor and he phoned the fire department. We did what we could with garden hoses until they arrived.

They found that four small fires had been set, and they literally chopped the place apart, with their fire fighting equipment. The owner was an old widow lady who had bought the house, paid to much for it, and couldn't make the payments, so tried the best thing that she could think of to get free of her overwhelming debt.

She then went across town to have coffee with her sister, hoping that her problem would go up in smoke. While we were still there the fire chief started questioning her. When I saw the look on her face I truly felt,

"Why couldn't I have arrived a couple hours later and sparred her the humiliation and grief she later had to endure."

One day a horseshoeing man told me that I had been born and lived in the best years ever in the world's history. I had some doubt. However when I look back he may have been right as I can't imagine the world changing as much in the future, as in the past.

As we travel down this trail of life sometimes many have had to burn the candle on both ends to get by.

When the Big Guy drops the gate into Heaven, I sincerely hope that he will let in those of us, who have been rebels at one time or another, during our lifetime.

Dusty Roundup

Chapter 13
Fish

Bob Fisher was an old style cowboy, who came from a Christian family. He was known as Fish by most of the community. In later years I came to know Bob and was privileged to become a friend, always calling him Fish. He was born north of the Neutral Hills into a fairly large family. It was a ranching area but the family did not have much range, cattle or money. At an early age he started cowboying.

I don't know much about his earlier years but I imagine that many calves from the old milk cows got ridden for entertainment. Fish turned pro at an early age and entered many small time rodeos. Often the winning didn't equal the entry fees. So he and three other young cowboys went state side to try their luck. They rode flatcars and anything that would get them to the next rodeo. Most times all they carried with them was a small war bag with the necessities of life, plus their saddle. The Bucking Association Saddle they guarded with their lives, as it was the only tool of their trade.

Fish chose Saddle Bronc Riding because he said that it was the cleanest event of the sport. He rode to a third place finish at Madison Square Gardens, and also a third place finish in Boston where he won a fancy Silver Tea Set. He said that he didn't win any major championships, but did win a lot of Silver Belt Buckles. These he said came in handy to keep his pants up when the grub got really short. For a traveling cowboy that was pretty often the case.Fish was a tall lanky, narrow waisted man, who always wore blue jeans, tight pointed cowboy boots and a big Western Stetson Hat. He looked like a Western cowboy off the range, not some dude type out off the movies. He worked for several years on ranches in New Mexico to hone his skills.

Fish had a way with words that was so entertaining. He also was a gentleman who tipped his hat to the ladies and never did I ever hear him swear or use the "F" word.

I was quite young when I first saw him ride a bronc. He had come back up north to compete. He told of how he had earned $4500 dollars that winter. This was a small fortune in those days.

When the rodeo announcer would say, "Bob Fisher, from the Neutral hills out of chute number such and such" the crowd would become silent in anticipation. When they cracked the gate Bob had his spurs over the shoulder on the first jump. To watch him spur in rhythm with the horse bucking was like poetry in motion. Most of the broncs of the day had never seen a man before, let alone have one sitting on them and spurring. There were many wild and wooly rides.

Nowadays a cowboy can go on the web, or phone a friend and find out the bucking pattern of all the rodeo stock.

After the eight second ride, in would ride Jim Todd, the pickup man on his pick-up bay gelding named Scotty. He was the strongest man I ever knew that never trained or pumped iron. He could pick off a cowboy at arms length, just like a feather and set them down gently on the ground, as if the rider was an expensive vase.

The crowds would go wild. Fish would just tip his hat and act as if it was just another Sunday ride in the pasture. Another trademark of Fish was that he always had his thumb pointed straight up in the air while gripping his buck shank.

As he grew older he did a lot of judging. One time a cowboy contestant came limping into the area carrying his rigging. Everybody thought how tough he was still competing with a broken leg. Fish just drawled, "If he broke his other leg you wouldn't even notice his limp."

Fish gradually slowed down to working his small ranch. He would visit his neighbors for coffee and tell stories, some with varying degrees of truthfulness.

One day I had taken a load of feed down to a mill customer. Clayton and Fish were discussing the merits of Clayton's new saddle horse. To be truthful, Clayton didn't want to ride him, as the horse was a little "edgy". So Fish throws his old saddle on the horse, tightens the cinch, and climbs aboard. Down goes the horses' head, as he took to bucking squealing and passing a lot of gas. On the first trip around the corral Fish hollers to Clayton "How much did you pay for this nag?" "$ 1200 dollars," was reply's Clayton.

On the second round Fish yells back, "You paid too much." After about four trips around the corral of furious bucking, up comes the horses head. Fish was in total control, and could make that horse do anything he asked him too. That cowboy was at least seventy years old at the time. I guess that the horse knew that he had a great rodeo rider on his back. Fish stepped off and said, "I'll shorten the stirrups, and you can try him Clayton." To which Clayton replied, "No way. This outlaw is going back to the next horse sale, let's go in for coffee."

We went into the house where Fish sauntered over to the kitchen and helped himself to coffee and a piece of cake. After taking a bite teasingly said, "I should have eaten this cake last week, it's a little dry this week." Lila was really a wonderful cook and took no offence to his dry humor.

Fish would always come up to the feed mill to get his little bottle of Doctor Bell's wonder medicine. He claimed that if you soaked a toothpick in it, and then chewed on it, that you would never get a cold. This stuff was terrible tasting. I gave some to a cat one time and we didn't see the cat again for three days.

One of my favorite stories that he told me was about the early years on the ranch. He and his two younger brothers Clarence and Skinny had to go out to the barn to feed the horses. This was about a quarter mile from the house. One of the worst blizzards in history blew in. It lasted for three days, and three nights. They were storm stayed out in the barn.

Then he drawled, "And the women had to bring us out our meals." Fish loved the ranch life, and enjoyed the branding get together, where cowboys could visit and swap lies. I was talking to Fish one day at an auction sale when a young neighbor lad came up and asked him if he could come over next week and give him a hand at branding. Fish looks at him, nonchalantly, picks his nose, examines it on his finger and drawls,

"I guess that I'm not too busy that day if I can recall my daybook."

He lived in a little shack north of the Neutral Hills. I asked him once if he was ever married, to which he replied, "Yeah I tried that once but will never do that again."

In his shack he had an old wooden cook stove that had the top bent down in the middle. Apparently he was cooking beans in a pressure cooker and it exploded. There were still beans embedded in the ceiling eight years later.

In 1991 the local paper came out to interview him about his rodeo career and asked him about how he won his Silver Tea set. It was quite a story.

He didn't apologize for his bachelor house, he just drawled, "The cleaning lady just stepped out in 85, but I expect her back any time now." Fish did not live too far from the Gooseberry Lake Gas Plant, which supplied him with natural gas. On some of the coldest mornings he would phone over and say, "Boys it's pretty cold over here do you think somebody could come by and check the gas flow and get the heat going again?"

Most of the fellows loved an excuse to go over, have coffee and listen to his stories. That's how the little story came to light that Fish had lived through the hungry thirties depression and didn't waste any food. He had been making use of a lot of road kill that they saw hanging in this old lean too.

One night he was coming home in his truck and saw a big jack rabbit lying dead on the road. He slowed down, opened the truck door and reached down to grab the rabbit by the ears. The problem was that the rabbit was frozen down to the road, and when he grabbed it, he was jerked right out of the truck cab. Luckily he wasn't going too fast, but was pulled out of the truck, which went on, and into the snow filled ditch. In his cowboy boots and hat, he walked a long cold half-mile to a neighbors to get a tow. It was about 30 below and he had a big graze on his cheek. He "fessed up" to what had happened, and another Fish story was born.

When we ran our feed mill at the ranch friday was Auction Market Day. After the sale was over, a lot of ranchers would drop by for their supplies, free coffee and some of Diane's home baking. They always seemed to solve all the problems of the world, and even some of their neighbor's problems. One day one of the men said, "Fish I'm sorry to hear about your sister Kate having a stroke. Is she bedridden now?" Fish takes a sip of coffee and drawls, "No she still sleeps alone."

When we moved away from that area we kind of lost track of a lot of those colorful people. In the local paper we read that Fish had passed away peacefully. I was glad for him because there would not have been a strong enough corral in any Seniors Lodge to hold this wandering old cowboy.

I'll bet that when we all get to heaven we will see a bunch of angels all laughing, and know that Fish is in the midst of them drawling out another Fish yarn.

CHAPTER 14
WAR

Every year as Remembrance Day draws near, I give a few personal thoughts as to why mankind seems to enjoy killing each other. A fellow once told me that it is the biggest buzz you can ever have, to shoot at somebody. I guess that is why they have paint ball games.

Many Christians, and non-Christians have been killed in wars because people were ordered to kill each other. The dead may have eternal life, but knew that they would not rise again in three days. My dad who had many sayings often said, "When you are dead… you are dead as the Dutchman's dog". I guess that was his way of saying that he didn't believe in eternal life.

Can you imagine the starving people being marched into the gas chambers by the thousands? The pain and suffering these people endured must have been horrific, and we today, cannot even imagine it. This has gone on for centuries and I am sure that in this group Adolf Hitler's name would come to mind first. However, he did bring the world out of a financial depression, at the cost of millions of lives. So was he a villain, or a hero?

Many of the soldiers that I remember in the Second World War joined up because they had no jobs, and no money. They would get a uniform, lots to eat, and the girls all loved a man in uniform.

As the war went on there were many deserters, good people too, that just didn't want to go, and to kill. There were also religious pacifists, for example the Hutterites, who stayed home, and farmed. They expanded their farmland and paid no taxes, until recent years.

When conscription came, everybody went to war, except some farm boys, that had to stay back to raise food for the troops. The women were encouraged to join the forces to manufacture clothes, bullets, and build war machinery.

I remember two cases of deserters in our area. One young fellow was stooking bundles for a neighbor of ours. The R.C.M.P. came out and took him away. The other story involved a very mean R.C.M.P, whom nobody liked, who came to collect this young lad. His mother met the policeman at the door and laid him out cold with a cast iron frying pan, picked him up, and threw him behind the old kitchen wood stove. She was boiling up water to pour on him when the younger brothers came home and stopped her. This was an extreme case, but she did not want her son to be killed.

World War I and II were the wars that would supposedly end all wars, and where are we today? We are still fighting over oil, money, power, and other things people are jealous about.

On the humorous side, our neighbor always told the story about his friend that was in the paratroopers with him. They were flying over enemy territory, the troops were told to jump out of the plane, yell "Geronimo" then pull the rip cord, and the chute would open. When Norman's turn came, he jumped out. All of a sudden there was a banging on the plane door. Upon opening there was Norman hanging on by one hand shouting, "What was that Indian's name again?"

No matter what we think of wars, it always seems to bring something good out of the heartache and misery. However, we should be able to do things without always killing each other.

This Remembrance Day let's honor the brave men and women who fought for freedom, and what they believed was right.

After the war many veterans came home crippled, both physically and mentally, with no help from the Government. Some retuned to their land, but found farming to be a pretty dull life, so entered into other occupations.

In the world of farming, it was the beginning of the mechanical revolution. Big tractors, ploughs and discs were coming into use, and horses were becoming obsolete. You didn't have to rest a tractor or feed it. This wasn't the best for the farmer as he could now work 18 to 20 hours a day, and the tractor never tired. We had one field of 100 acres that we had purchased from a neighbor, who used to farm with a small tractor, and a six-foot cultivator. When he summer fallowed it, by the time he got completely over it, the weeds were already coming up where he had started the field a couple of weeks or more ago. Now, we could pull into that same field with the big tractor and cultivator and pull out again in three hours time.

One time in that same field I was out working alone and got my tractor stuck. I hooked the tractor onto the big truck with a long chain. I then went back, put the stuck tractor into the lowest gear so the wheels were turning in the mud. I ran ahead, jumped into the big grain truck and pulled the tractor out of the mud hole and onto a dry piece of ground. I then jerked the truck out of gear, quickly jumped out and ran back to stop the tractor before it crashed into the back of the truck.

One man could farm many more acres, and along with scientific developments, a lot of plant and animal diseases were brought under control. One example of this was blackleg in cattle, which caused many losses. Your animals could look healthy at night, but by morning any number could be dead. The only way that you could know the cause was to rub your hand over the shoulder of the dead animal. If you heard a crinkly sound you knew that it was blackleg. This was a soil born disease and could live for years in the soil. You never hear of it anymore because of vaccine.

Another pest that could cause you a big expense but that never killed an animal was the warble fly. It would lay it's eggs on the feet of a cow (hence called heel fly). The grub would work it's way up to the back of the animal, and would come out of a puss filled lesion on the meat of the back as a grub. It would then fall to the ground where it would hatch, and the life cycle would start all over again. The biggest loss was all the sores and the holes in the hide of the animal.

So now if anyone says to me, that they want only "all natural" I just say, "Would you sooner have a warble grub in your meat?" Thank goodness we are warble free now because of science.

People nowadays can look on a date on some food produce then say, "It's a day old I can't eat that."

Years ago when there was smut and rust in the cereal crops, every machine would either be black or red. The grain kernels would look like little mouse "turds." Your income would be nothing for that year as you could not sell it, or ever feed it to your animals. I guess that is why we still have disagreements amongst people. For example, a young lady walks into a grocery store wearing a $180 pair of designer jeans to complain about the price of milk going up 5 cents. It just does not seem to make sense!

There will always be problems with some food and drinks, which we should be aware of. However, with science and common sense our life expectancy is getting longer. I really believe that the human population is not doing too badly in making our standard of living acceptable.

Backs against the Blizzard

CHAPTER 15
THE UNACCLAIMED LEGEND

Throughout history we have heard great stories of cowboys and folk heroes. Wyatt Erp, Billy the Kid, and Wild Bill Hickcock, only to mention a few.

They became legends of their time. Did you ever notice that they all came from south of the border?

The Czar area in East Central Alberta has long been known to have produced more than their share of good cowboys, and Billy Mc Lean was one of the finest. Besides being a good cowboy, Billy was an extremely colorful character.

Billy Mc Lean was born at Kitscoty on June 24, 1921. It seemed that he was destined to be a cowboy practically from the time he could walk. His first trip to Czar was in 1937 when he and Russ Greenwood trailed bucking horses from Kitscoty to the famous Czar Stampede, a ninety-mile trip.

Later Billy bought a ranch in the area and settled there between rodeos. Billy worked all the events at the rodeos, unlike the specialized one-event cowboys of today. His best event was Saddle Bronc Riding for which he collected many awards. In 1949, Billy McLean won the Canadian All Around Championship. That same year he competed against the American Cowboys at the Calgary Stampede and won the All Around Championship there. A feat equal today, to winning the Las Vegas National World Title.

Some of the Czar people he rodeoed with were the Laye Brothers, Billy Brown, Bob, Skinny and Clarence Fisher, Bud Brooks, and Jim

Todd, who was the strongest pickup man I have ever known. He could pick a man off a bucking bronc at full arms length and set him gently down on the ground.

His former friends and competitors always told that Billy had a kind heart second to none. He was always willing to help the beginning cowboy and he never forgot you when you were down. He was a very proud and self-sufficient man.

Billy McLean did have one fault; he liked to over indulge at times. And during some of these escapades, many pretty interesting things happened.

In the Czar History Book, Billy wrote, "the Czar stampedes at the lake used to last a couple days after the rodeo." This was very true.

He owned an ugly brown horse called Hammer Head, who they say could drink as much beer as Billy. Now that took some doing. He would ride Hammer Head from his ranch four miles right into the Czar Bar for a cool one. Another day he rode six miles to Hughenden, and right inside the restaurant. Billy refused to leave until the poor excited non-English speaking Chinese lady, served Hammerhead sugar lumps.

One late evening Billy entered the Czar Bar wearing his Six Gun and announced that he was going to shoot his neighbor for looking at is wife. He twirled his Six Shooter, and with two shots, he shot out the lights. It was too dark to see the neighbor, who by then had hastily disappeared out the back door.

The hotel man calmly lit some old lanterns and continued to serve drinks to all his customers, including Billy.

He used to do some outriding for Rod Bullock's Chuckwagon, and while at the Calgary Stampede in the 50's, he ended up in one of the biggest chuckwagon wrecks in history.

A chuckwagon went down in front of him. His horse slammed into the wagon and catapulted Billy right over the wagon, and the lead team. He was unconscious and Wayne Vold pulled him off the track by his boots. He woke up the next day in the hospital with a broken neck. When the chuckwagon driver who had caused the wreck came up to see him, Billy asked, "What did you stop there for?"

Less than a decade later he had another accident while showing some neighbor kids how to ride a boys bike, while putting his leg through the frame. This ended with a badly broken leg and traction for many months.

He used to entertain and cheer up many a patient and nurse in the hospital with his wit and stories. On Saturday nights some of his old cronies would always come to see him. It soon became known that they were sneaking in a few refreshments, but as long as things didn't get out of hand, the staff would tend to look the other way. However, one evening after the group had left, Billy kept getting louder and louder. The nurse who was on duty at the time went in to search for the hootch, but could find nothing.

She asked him to please quieten down because there was an extremely sick lady in the next room who was dying.

Billy was so sorry, and agreed to be quiet.

He was...for a while. He felt so sorry for the poor lady that he started to sing hymns to see her home. "Jesus Loves Me" and "Lead Me Gently Home Father" were sung reverently, but very loudly.

In marched the nurses to conduct a more thorough search. The firewater was found..... in the bedpan. He had poured it into the bedpan, so no one would find it, and had been drinking out of it all night.

Billy moved south to Monitor, ranched for a few years and later settled at Sundre.

As the years passed his strong muscles weakened, from the many years on the rodeo trail. He was a proud man who prided himself on making his way in life without being dependent on anyone.

His eyes used to sparkle as he reminisced and relived the excitement of his rodeo days.

Billy suffered a very severe stroke, and was placed on the Life -Support System. When he later regained consciousness the Doctor explained to him what had happened.

The next day October 24, 1986, Billy McLean died. We were told that he had been able to gather enough strength to unplug his own Life Support System!

You know it wasn't a surprise to those who knew him to find how he had taken the situation at hand and done what he felt was best, on that final ride over the ridge.

I don't know if Billy scored an 85 in God's big arena of life, or if he got the yellow flag. But I'll bet that on his way out he tipped his Stetson to the crowd and walked out in his high-heeled boots, his spurs jingling, a true independent cowboy.

Billy McLean was quietly laid to rest at Lloydminster, Alberta. A horses head adorns his tombstone.

CHAPTER 16

HALLOWEEN

In the olden days Halloween sometimes got a little out of hand, as some of the tricks and no treats became legalized vandalism. Lets take a look back in time to when some of the so-called kids could get a buggy up on top of a Hip Roof Barn, in the middle of a dark night. It is a mystery how they could get it done quietly, so that no one even heard what happened. The next day it would take the owner some time trying to get it down in one piece.

At one farm the owner thought that he heard a noise and went out to investigate. Someone threw a lasso over him, jerked his feet out from under him, and he was tied up in less than seven seconds. He was left there for most of Halloween night until some family member missed him. They went out to the yard and sure enough there he was tied up nicely with hay bales piled around him, so he wouldn't get cold.

Padding the church bell with old clothes, so as to silence it, sounds pretty minor, but took a lot of dangerous high climbing to accomplish.

Probably one of the funniest acts happened in a small prairie town. A string of flat cars had been spotted on the siding for days. On Halloween night a group of pranksters collected and loaded many of the villagers old outhouses on the flat car. Unfortunately during the night the train stopped and picked up that string of cars loaded with the biffys, and proceeded down the main line to Wilkie Sask. This was the divisional point, where with a roundhouse, the shipments to the rest of Canada were staged from there. The next day before the cars were shipped onward someone noticed and wired the small town to see if they were missing some of their outhouses. They were given 24 hours to come and retrieve them. This was about a 200 mile roundtrip and of course many did not have a vehicle worthy of traveling that distance, or hauling a biffy. It was a community effort but most eventually retrieved their necessary outhouse. On the long trip home no one had to worry about finding a rest stop.

There was a fellow in town, who always had trouble finding the out house at night, especially after consuming a dozen or so suds at the local bar. His wife sized up a plan to help him in the dark. She had him memorize,

"Count 30 steps along the fence, then do a hard right, and go 5 more steps, you then should be able to reach out and feel the door catch."

The man said later. "I shouldn't have taken that 6th step because by then my outhouse was probably 20 miles down the C.P.R. tracks."

The old biffys seemed to get the worst of most of the Halloween pranks. Some people knew that it would be probably be tipped, so the smart ones would move their own toilet about half the length of the hole. I remember one poor fellow, the lead prankster, who got there first and he fell head first into the hole. Needless to say he had to ride in the back of the truck the rest of the night.

We lived a long way out in the country so were never bothered much. One particular night the power was switched off and the dogs started to bark. I went out and heard a bunch of laughing and giggling coming from back up on the hill road. I walked up the road to where their vehicle was parked and got in and sat and waited until they came back. There were some pretty shocked kids when they opened the truck door and there I was in the drivers seat. I knew all of them, and they just about fell over each other saying, "We didn't do anything but move a few gates. I quietly said "that's fine, now if you will all come into the house Diane will have the R. C. M. P. on the phone." I thought that some of them would jump and run but they all came in liked whipped dogs. Low and behold there was hot chocolate and cookies for them on the table. Talk about happy and relieved kids.

One neighbor girl raised rabbits. Somehow somebody got into the hutch and spray- painted them all different colors.

If you had a tame old milk cow she would usually be tied on the deck, with a horse caller and harness on her, or maybe your best saddle. Another favorite was to fill a truck cab up with turkeys, chickens, or maybe a stinking old billy goat if one was available. There was always something to laugh about after Halloween, and some new pranks to think about for next year.

One other trick happened at a tiny post office. Some how the pranksters got in and turned an Emu loose. It sorted the mail, crapped on everything, stamped the letters, and was really on the fight by the time someone found it. No one dared to go inside, as an Emu can be very vicious when confined. They had to leave the door open and after awhile he wandered out and left town. I'll bet that he didn't get far before the postmaster shot him.

One other Halloween the small boys greased the railroad tracks in our local town. It all started in the afternoon when there was a discussion amongst the young folk about all the old tricks that had been tried, and how it was time for some new ones. The idea came up to grease the railroad tracks, so every guy there went home and got as much grease or oil as they could carry. Even the used oil behind the old Esso service station was carted off. These kids worked long and hard with their wooden spoons and sticks to grease a long stretch of track in front of the station.

The old steamer train would puff into town at a certain time and a small crowd would gather on the station platform to watch. The engineer would always give a little toot on the whistle and then apply the brakes. This time when he gave the little toot and applied the brakes nothing happened. The harder he applied the brakes, the faster the train seemed to go. Although the brakes were locked, the old steamer seemed to gather speed until the heavy steel wheels hit the cold dry steel tracks. Then the sparks flew in all directions. You could smell the burning oil and grease all over town. The guilty kids thought,

"Oh my God we've gone to far this time," and they all headed out in different directions. The adults stood looking in shock.

After a lot of spinning backwards the train came to a stop in front of the station. The engineer climbed down in a rage and swore that every kid that was responsible would get, "20 years of hard labor and 6 lashes a day." He then climbed back into the cab and after a lot of spinning in the hot grease the train left town. This was a prank that people talked and laughed about for years. Nobody every told who had done the oiling.

Halloween in Metiskow

Chapter 17

Trucks

Transportation has always been of the utmost importance for the people living a fair ways from town. My uncle had an old 1 ½ ton Ford truck, which you had to always double clutch, and kind of herd down the road.

I guess that it wasn't to valuable as he would let us drive it, long before we had a driver's license. Which reminds me, I never took a drivers test until I was 60 years old, for a class one license that I needed to drive my new Volvo Tractor to pull a B Train. I passed it the first try. We used it to hall canola, grain, fertilizer, and other goods.

I had never pulled a cattle liner before, so when a friend of mine asked me to help him get a load of fats from Beaver Lodge, west of Grande Prairie to haul down to Cargill at High River, I said O.K. and met him at the Aldersyde Truck stop east of our place. He crawled into the sleeper and said, "you drive while I rest!'

It was an adventure taking it through the Calgary traffic, and heading north. We left at 11 o'clock at night and were back at the plant by 7p.m. the next evening. When hauling livestock you just don't stop except for a bathroom break. A trip like that soon takes the romance out of wheeling one of those big tractors down the road, and imagining that everyone is envying you.

However, this trip turned out much better than years ago when I drove my first truck out of town. My dad had bought a brand new 2 ton Mercury truck. It was the first new vehicle that we had ever had on the farm. We were going to build the box, and had the box lumber loaded on the back, plus a 16 foot steel rod tied to it. There was a red flag tied on the end of it all. I was meeting a car on the bridge, when BANG, this women hits me in the back. She was a speed demon and had her left leg in a cast, and was handling the clutch, break and foot feed, all with her right foot. She was about to pass me on the bridge, when she saw another car coming, and she wheeled in behind me at a terrific speed. The back of the truck, plus my seat where smashed in against the steering wheel. It was tight, but I could still get out. The women, was lucky too, as the rod went right through her windshield, and steering wheel spokes, and her seat. She had seen the red flag, and rod coming at her and ducked, or it would have gone right through her chest.

I had just gotten my drivers license, and it was terrible start to have your Dad's new truck in a wreck, and the R.C.M.P. trying to say that you shouldn't have had that rod sticking out the back. However, after the truck was fixed it spent many useful years of service at our place.

During my life time, I had quite a few different trucks, but the one that I spent the most time in was a Big C cab 800 Dodge, with a long box for hauling cattle, which we called Big Red.

The idea came to me one night as I was writing out ear tags with a jiffy pen, while waiting for a heifer to calve. We had just paid a trucker to haul some cattle, and I was doing the math on the side of a Spanbolette box (sulfur pills for pneumonia).

It looked pretty promising, and if I quit smoking as well, it was sure to be a money maker. So, with all that math done on the side of the medicine box, I took it in to our banker to see if a loan could be worked out.

I guess he thought that if I quit smoking that I'd live long enough to pay off the loan, so he said yes. The next day we went to Edmonton and bought the truck.

One small thing that ticked me off right from the start, was the 16 gallon fuel tank. The truck did 6 miles to the gallon. We lived 200 miles from Edmonton, so we had to install a big extra fuel tank. Next were all the gears. You could double clutch, and then there was a short sift. I swear that somebody had a bunch of extra gears, threw them into the transmission case, and quickly bolted the gearshift down. However, I finally got all the gears figured out and started in on the money making aspect of trucking.

There was a small packing plant in Edmonton called Inercontinental Packers, that really liked the way we finished our steers. The problem was that they would always want our fats for the morning kill by about 7:30 a.m. It was 200 miles from our place, so at 2 o'clock in the morning, I would load the cattle, Diane would pack me a lunch, and I was on the road. If you were lucky you might see a rabbit stupid enough to be out at that time of night. Talk about distracted driving, I drank more coffee and ate more sandwiches, than any coffee shop could serve, while still driving down the highway, with a load of cattle on.

We did many jobs with Big red. One time when our son Jay was a baby we went out to Rocky Mountain House to visit our relatives, and bring home a load of lumber. Diane laughed and said that the old truck made 50 miles to a diaper. The fun part of that trip was when the truck was fully loaded the front wheels didn't have much weight on them. We hit some rough road and ended up facing the wrong way on the highway. It just swung right around on the back wheels. I believe that the whole family could have used a diaper change about then.

It was fun too, as when the kids were little and we had an eight track, plus a C.B. put in. On the pasture hauls we'd all belt out "Old Strawberry Roan," and many others. What we lacked in being in tune, we made up for in volume. Wilf Carter was famous on our ranch!

There were some close calls, which are a normal part of being on the road a lot. Probably the worst scare that I ever had was coming home with heavy load of 20 foot steel eye beams that were 12 inches wide. I had the truck wide open while coming around the big curves at Sedgewick, Alberta. Four school buses were crossing the highway. Three of them stopped and crossed. The 4th one stopped and attempted to cross in front of me. I don't know if the sun was in her eyes or what but she pulled into the center of the road, saw me, threw up her arms, and slammed on the brakes. I had no time to decide, but knew that I couldn't hit a school bus broad side. I also knew that if I hit the ditch the beams would take me, and the cab off. I knew that I couldn't stop, so I shot by her with my right wheels just grazing the ditch shoulder. I whipped by, said a short prayer, and kept on trucking for home.

Another time I had left again about 2 o'clock in the morning and delivered the cattle to Edmonton, then headed to Buck Lake for a load of fence posts. Paul Kramer was a great guy, and I had hauled posts from him for at least ten years. When I arrived he'd always say, come on in for some lunch and we'll visit while the men load. I never had to count the posts because he would never short you, but he never gave you any extra posts. He was one honest man. With over 100 miles of fence we had many visits. I was heading home and getting pretty sleepy, when on comes the cops light behind me. I pulled over, stopped, and rolled down the window. The young R.C.M.P. jumped up and stuck his head in the truck cab, and took a couple of sniffs to see if I had been drinking.

He said, "How long have you been driving cowboy."

I replied, "Quite awhile".

He continued, "You know that you have been weaving quite a bit? I won't give you a ticket if you promise to stop at the camp site down the road and have a sleep".

That was a "no brainer" so pulled into the campsite where a little car was parked.

Now if you didn't let the truck idle a bit before you turned the key off it would back fire. I just cruised in, and turned off the key. There was two of the loudest bangs you ever heard.

There was a little man in the car sleeping. He leapt out of the car and was heading for the open country as fast as his short legs would carry him. Before he reached the road he glanced back and saw that it was just a truck. He stopped, turned around and came back and shook his fists at me before getting in his car and leaving. I really didn't care, just locked the doors and fell asleep. Another time I had been making too many trips, without stopping. I pulled into the set of lights at Fort Road in Edmonton. It was one of those long sets of lights, and I dozed off. The other vehicles honking soon brought me around.

I used to sometimes stop for coffee at a truck stop west of Camrose. One time I was there an old neighbor pulled in ahead of me with his three loads of straights, and a body job. He must of had a good price quoted, as when he entered the coffee shop he announced in a loud voice, "steaks for everybody on me". Just then the body job missed the turn approach, and tipped over spilling out all the cattle. He ran out to look, and then ran back in and said, "change that order to hamburgers."

We used that old red Dodge for many years, and never had a road accident. We lived on a side hill, and one time had backed it out of the shop and parked it. It was glare ice on the side hill, and sometime during the night a strong wind came up and shook the truck badly, and caused it to slide. It ended up sliding under a 1000 gallon fuel tank, which came down on it. The total front end was smashed and the frame was bent. Our insurance company wrote it off, and that was the end of Big Red.

I didn't make a fortune as planned, but I did stay off cigarettes.

Riding out

CHAPTER 18
LARRY

Larry came to work at our place just after school finished for the year. He was probably an average student academically, but school just didn't interest him. He was a tall lanky fellow and very good-natured. Most people liked him because he could talk and laugh his way out of most situations.

I always said that he was half-man and half-boy, because one week he'd come to work with a pocket full of cigarettes, and the next week he'd have pockets full of candies. Man could he eat! If there was a roast chicken or roast beef, and he was the first to the table there wouldn't be much left for anybody else but bones, yet he never gained a pound.

One morning I went into town to pick him up for work. His mother met me at the door and said that he'd be right out, but asked if I could give him work where he didn't have to sit down. Of course I said, "how come?"

She started to explain and burst out laughing so hard, that the tears were streaming down her cheeks. In between the gales of laughter, she told that Larry came home late, and had gone out to the old unused back house. He lit up his cigarette, and settled down for a nice little "relaxational." The nest of wasps under the seat didn't like having their lights shut out so went to work with their stingers. Even in the dark they still could hit the bull's eye. Larry came screaming across the yard with his pants around his ankles, flailing with his arms at the wasps, and trying to get his pants up, the swarm of wasps following him. His mother said, "I don't know what happened in there, but the wasps seemed awfully upset."

Larry recovered from this and in about a week, the haying operation got underway. I had very small haying equipment then, just a couple small tractors with no cabs, a rake and baler. I put Larry on the hay rake putting two rounds together so the baler could handle it. One day I looked across the field and there he was smoking and whistling, driving the tractor with no rake behind. It had become unlooked, and he hadn't noticed. I stopped my tractor, stepped up on the tractor wheel and waved at him. He just waved back at me and kept going. He then came up upon his unhooked rake, and wondered who would leave a rake in the middle of the hay field. As he pulled out to go around it, he noticed that he didn't have a rake behind his tractor. What a joke it was. He was laughing and smoking and said, "I wondered why you were so friendly today waving all the time."

Larry progressed quickly on machinery and by harvest time he was running the tractor and baler. We put seventeen thousand square bales through that machine two years in a row. After harvest, we then had to haul them home and stack them by hand in the yard. I had developed a knack with a long handled fork, that I could pitch a bale up onto the high 3-ton truck box with no effort. Larry would then stack the bales high above the truck box. We would drive home to the stack. I would pitch the bales off and we would build the bales into a high stack.

When we had all the bales in a long neat stack he used to laugh and say, "Boy it takes two men to see from one end of the stack to the other." As Larry grew older he really wanted to be a cowboy but seemed to have a lot of stomach trouble.

Not enough guts!

One day he brought in a young colt that he wanted to break for one of his girlfriends. The colt had been spoiled and would pull back on the halter, until either the halter broke or you untied it. Then it would just rear up and fall over backwards.

I said, "that horse will go over backward on you and break you up, or worse yet kill you, so let's try it this way. "You snub it to a post and when it starts to pull back, I'll jump on it's neck and ear it down. Then you can put the saddle on and mount up."

I was chewing on the horse's ear and Larry finally got it saddled, which seemed to take forever, as the colt was really getting restless. I spat out a bunch of horsehair and said,

"Get on you so and so chicken".

I glanced back and there was Larry one toe up in the stirrup, and the other leg trembling like a leaf in the wind. Then he said, "Hold it a little longer I have to pee" and ran around the corner of the barn.

I guess that the colt had enough training for one day as it gave a mighty heave and sent me flying to the ground, and took to bucking and bellowing around the corral. Larry came out from behind the barn looking a little pale saying,

"You know if you could have held it a little longer, I think I could have ridden it."

I just said, "If you had lifted your other leg, the way you were shaking your boot would have fallen off."

After we'd finished harvest those few years Larry went to work for other people and I didn't see him for quite awhile. One day he rode in with a pair of beautiful sorrel mares and worked on me to buy them. I said no and he left. However, he was back the next day saying he needed the money, and could I even buy one. He said that she was so well trained that you had to slap her on the side of the head to get her to turn. So I made him an offer, which he took immediately.

After he left I got thinking, "what if he stole this mare? She looked pretty well bred." I gave her a going over looking for brands and tattoos. Sometimes horses will be tattooed on the inside of the bottom lip. I found nothing, so the deal turned out to be a good one. Diane rode her sorrel horse Lady for many years.

Another time Larry drove into the yard and said, "I understand you are looking for some pipe to build corrals."

I said, "yes". He responded, "I'm your man, but instead of money I will trade you for two dry heifers to butcher." We agreed on the load of pipe, and with a laugh he added, "I'm going to beat you on this deal you know."

So I just said, "go ahead there has to be a first for you sometime."

For some reason I ended up in the hospital for a couple of days, and Larry and this great big Indian showed up to butcher the animals. Diane knew which animals he was to get, so helped get them into the small corral, then retreated to the house.

The first thing they did was drive the truck and stock trailer into the corral, then took out two big bottles of whiskey and a case of beer and set them on the hood. They couldn't seem to decide who should shoot the animals, but after a couple beer, and a few slugs of whiskey, Larry did it. Instead of cutting the throats so the animals would bleed properly they had a few more shots of courage, with the animals lying there stone dead.

Once an animal stops moving, they will not bleed, and the blood stays in the meat. The next step is to get the hide off quickly and the intestines out or the gas will build up like a gas balloon.

This happened. So the Indian Brave stuck his big knifepoint into the gut and it exploded with a bang, covering both of them with blood and muck. After a couple more drinks, the smart thing to do was to shoot a hole in the other one to let the gas escape. By dark the job was done and the carcasses thrown into their dirty old stock trailer.

With empty bottles, they left and headed for the nearest town to get more courage, then back to the reservation.

I did get my pipes, but had to go away up north to Fox Creek, and then miles back into the bush. The pipe was all filled with cement and made a very heavy load. I'm sure that it was an abandoned well site and that the company was just happy to get the pipe cleaned up. It's a good thing that there were no weigh scales on the road home or I would have been fined for overloading.

I don't know which side got beaten on the deal, but my side was a lot cleaner and more sober.

I could write a book on Larry but will finish up with one more story. If you remember I mentioned that he loved ladies, and they loved him. One time a fellow came home earlier than was intended, and there was Larry's truck parked in front of his house late at night. This fellow was so mad that he hooked onto the truck with a chain and dragged it all over town honking his horn. The truck being in park, didn't allow the tires to turn, so all the tires burnt off. He then unhooked it, smashed the windows, and threw lit matches into the cab. I don't know what happened at the house, but Larry seemed to escape unhurt. No one even bothered to call the police.

One day I got a phone call from his mother asking if I would be a pallbearer, as Larry had passed away suddenly.

Some people thought he was a useless rogue, others said that he was a great guy.

To me, he was Just Larry, and that's the way I remembered him when we gathered to say goodbye.

Still Training Horses

CHAPTER 19
THE SEVENTIES

Back in the seventies there seemed to be more money around. There were better cattle and grain prices, and the expenses didn't seem to take every last cent out of your old blue jeans.

We desperately needed a new car on the ranch. Our local dealer told us that if we flew to the plant in Windsor, Ontario, and picked it up, that we could save $3,000. So we ordered a Plymouth Sport Fury, 2 door, dark blue, with a black vinyl roof.

The Toronto Royal Winter Fair was on, so we booked our flight. It was my first flight and I had some doubts about cramming 300 people in this long aluminum cylinder. It was quite different with the stewardesses walking up and down the aisle asking, "Sir would you care for a Drink?"

This was the first time in my life I had been called Sir. In the old hotels at home, the server would come up with the foaming tray, and just say, "You Cowboys ready for another round?" They didn't wait for a yes or a no, they just covered the table with tall glasses.

We landed safely in Toronto and spent a few days at the fair. The best livestock in North America were on display there, and it was very impressive to us country folk.

It was then on to the car factory to pick up our new car. It looked better in real life than on the brochures. With my wife all dressed up and me in my new Stetson and cowboy boots, I thought that we would surely set some new fashion standards at home, going to town or to church. That was a fond hope, all they said was,

"That old so and so must of done well on his fats"

We herded our new car home through all the major cities and never put a scratch on it. The first time we went to town at home some lady backed into it, and put a dent in the fender. We never did know who it was, but always felt that it would have been cause for justifiable homicide.

Back home on the ranch reality set in pretty quickly as calving season was about to start. I have never figured out why if you locked 6 cows in the barn at night because they look real "calvy," 5 others would go off the straw, and have their baby in a snow bank.

We had a large corral to feed, and to calve out the cows, and ear tag the calves. There were no yard lights, just you and the flashlight, and a few big trees to duck behind for protection. When a cow goes into labor her disposition seems to change, and you never know what she will do. Sometimes on those cold nights I would be chasing the cows through the trees, or they would be chasing me. This may sound a little primitive, but everyone was in the same boat.

Nowadays there is a T.V. in the barn and corral, so you can watch from your living room and zero in, if anything is in trouble. Most of us felt that we were lucky to have a T.V. in the house in those years, let alone in the barn.

If you lose a calf we would try to get a replacement. It was time consuming getting the cow to accept a new calf as her own, until we learned that if we skinned a sizable patch of hide from her dead calf, and then tied the skin on the new calf, she'd usually take it immediately. We called this, "The coat of many colors". The calf would wear this coat until the cow would accept the smell of the new calf, or until it eventually fell off.

Meanwhile, back at the ranch we were running low on replacement claves. However, during calving season there weren't enough of these babies for everyone. The Camrose Auction always had a lot of Holstein bull calves, as they were no good for the dairies, and the dairymen didn't want to bother feeding them. Can you believe that in some places in B.C. the dairymen gave their male calves away, or just destroyed them?

It was a nice spring Saturday so I suggested that we go for a drive in our new Fury to Camrose and see what calves were selling for.

My wife Diane said "You're not going to put a calf in our nice new car are you?"

I replied, "Of course not".......

But five calves went cheap, and we had to get them home.

It was simple, we had done it in the old car often. We would lie them down in the trunk of the car, then shut the lid. After a couple of minutes they'd realize that they couldn't stand up and lie quietly most of the time. It was roomy enough for them to assume their normal lying position.

We started herding these 5 baby calves to the car. A Good Samaritan came along to help us load. It wasn't bad getting number three and four in, while keeping numbers one and two down, but that 5th calf was tricky, to get the trunk closed before they all got up. My wife was the doorman and would shut the lid of the trunk, as the calves went in, before the others could get up. The Good Samaritan placed the fifth one in, as I tried to control the rest. I yelled, "Shut the lid! Shut the Lid!"

She did with full force, and there was the most awful thud.

I thought for a minute that the trunk lid had hit a calf on the head, but upon looking up, there was the poor Good Samaritan walking in a half dazed circle rubbing his head. Luckily he had his winter cap on, or I am sure that he would have had his head laid wide open.

Diane felt so badly and apologized profusely. We often wondered who the poor man was, how big a goose egg he developed, or after that if he ever offered to help anyone again.

We had many a laugh over the funny looks that the service station attendants would give us while filling the car with gas. A calf would bawl, or start to thump around. We'd be driving down the road and suddenly there'd be a moo, or a very unpleasant odor would drift forward. Then we had to drive a few miles with all the windows open, to air things out.

Blizzards can come up in hurry on the Prairies. By the time we had our calves loaded and gassed up, we were in the midst of a rip-roaring storm, and one hundred and twenty miles from home. We traveled in this massive storm, with high winds, blowing and falling snow. Turning off Highway 13 onto our ten miles of poor roads we struggled miraculously through drifts higher than the hood on the car. We made it to the creek-flat, one half mile from home, and there we became stuck to stay. I tried to shovel with a hub cap, but the wind was blowing the snow faster than I could shovel it away. I finally decided to walk home and come back with the tractor and manure spreader to get the calves and my wife.

The drifts were so high that I could only get back to within 300 yards of the car. We then proceeded to try to get the calves to the tractor, and spreader.

Long legged Holstein calves, who braced themselves with their front feet when you pushed them, so that all that would happen was that you'd lift their back end up into the air. Of course they didn't lead, and when you tried to pull them they braced all four feet. It was an exhausting episode pushing, pulling and carrying in three feet of drifting snow. We finally reached the tractor after many attempts. My wife had bought groceries, so they were loaded in the front, then the calves in the middle, and my dear wife Diane was stationed in a crouched position arms spread eagle to each side of the spreader, so that nothing fell out of the back. The beaters of the manure spreader had been removed, so we could haul silage, so there was nothing across the back end.

We started home with the small Massey Ferguson 35 Tractor and the manure spreader, which only had two wheels. When the tractor would stop and spin, the spreader would tilt down in front, and the calves would end up walking on the grocery bags. When the tractor would lounge ahead through the snow the calves would go back on my wife, who was trying to keep them in the manure spreader, as well as trying to keep them from stepping on her cold feet. But 5 calves had 20 sharp little feet, and the odds were not in Diane's favor.

The path that I had made coming out was of course by this time blown in, so we started again to make a trail, getting stalled, backing up, trying again, again and again—all the time the calves going back and forth from the groceries, to my wife, like a bubble in a level.

After what seemed like an eternity we made it back into the yard, got the calves into the warm barn, gave them a shot of penicillin, and headed for the house to warm up.

We could never remember being so cold in all our lives. When the feet and hands started to feel a bit warmer, then the chill-blains hit—severe cramps. All you could do was walk the floor in agony until they eased. Luckily we all recovered, and there wasn't even a sick calf.

The next day things seemed to settle down a bit, and the snow-plow came out. We got the new car unstuck and hauled home. Even though it was still −40 below the calves were coming along nicely.

That evening the phone rang. It was an old cattle buyer friend. He said,

"You remember last summer when you said you could use another 35 cows if the price was right. Well the price is right. Some have calves, and the cows do have long horns, and I'm sending them tomorrow," and hung up! The line went dead.

Some ranchers would buy old thin pregnant cows so they could sell the newborn calf, then fatten the cow up, and sell her for beef. The bigger the cow the better the packing plants liked them. It cost them the same amount to hang up a little cow, as it did a big one, but there was less dollar return to them.

These cows I had talked about buying last summer were coming tomorrow...... when I did not need replacement calves! They were from west of Wildwood and had long vicious horns to fight off the wolves and the coyotes.

The calves had sucked just before they were loaded into the dog box of the cattle liner. You can imagine the frostbite that the cows had on their wet tits, on a four and a half hour trip on the liner, with the wind whistling through the vent holes. They arrived about dark and the calves tried to suck. Every time a cold nose touched the cow, she would flail away with her feet like a windmill. The poor little calf would end up being kicked into a snow bank. I had to rope these cows one by one. It took a big loop to try to get the rope over these huge horns, and was very hard to do, especially in the dark. We had to tie up the cows back legs so she wouldn't kick, then drag up the calf to suck. You usually had to squirt out some milk first so the calf could smell it, before it would start sucking.

This was a slow and painful process, and so time consuming, until the idea hit me that I had just bought 5 mobile milk machines the day before in Camrose. Each old cow was tied up and never knew what hit her when those hungry Holsteins grabbed on for dinner. It was funny how even little animals catch on by sight. The calves could be dozing in a stall, and when they heard the rope swish through the air they were up and latched onto the cow before she was even snubbed up.

This routine lasted about two weeks until the cows healed up, and let their own babies nurse. It's strange we called these cows "bush cows," but with a little extra feed they turned out well, and produced calves for us for many years.

Fattening Cattle

Chapter 20
Sorting & Moving Cattle

It was the 20th of June and that's the day when we could put some of our cattle into the Wainwright Buffalo Park Grazing Association. This was part of the Wainwright Military Camp. In the earlier years before the drift fences were built the cattle grazed on over 30,000 acres between our place, highway 41, and the Army Camp. We didn't have to rotate the cattle, we just turned them out in June, after the army finished their exercises. The cattle would graze at free will wondering for miles. It was mostly sand hills, muskeg, and scrub bush.

One particular place that was always a mystery to me was the Rae Springs. It was a natural spring that bubbled right out of a sand hill. It was clear cold water, and very drinkable. We always stopped there to water our horses and ourselves. You could reach down up to your elbow and touch the bottom, which was hard as a rock. The cattle tramped around it as long as I can remember, and it was about three and one half feet wide, and always kept bubbling up. At one time three men sat in a square washtub in the spring and the bubbling kept them afloat. It is truly one of God's natural phenomena's in our part of the world.

We were able to run 150 cow calf pairs in the camp. They had to be branded and fly tagged before they went. For years we would run the main herd into our corral and then try to match mother and baby calf. What a job this was! One day I thought, "why can't they sort themselves?" I built a gate with an opening just big enough for the calves to come through. We would then gate run out the 150 cows that we wanted to go into the next small corral, and leave them overnight. The cows couldn't get back, so with the cows bawling, and their bags getting full of milk, the hungry calves would squeeze through my invention. They would be sorted and ready to move by the next morning. This turned out to be just about 100% effective.

This particular morning we started the herd drive at daybreak, as it was 10 miles to the park gate, and it would be very hot by noon. Diane and I hadn't been married too long at this time. She was riding her favorite mare Lady and I was riding Charlie Brown. Randy was riding old Rusty, and of course Jessie the Dog, our border collie was helping. We were several miles into the trip and Randy was leading the herd. Diane would watch the approaches and farmstead's without gates, and of course the Hutterite gardens along the way. We were moving along nicely. One neighbor had saddled up and was helping for a while. His old pony and equipment had seen better days. He was happy for a little ride, company and the B.S. He was a great water conservationist, he just never bothered wasting the water to wash! There was enough real estate in the wrinkles of his neck and face to plant a crop. His nephews referred to him as "Uncle Stinky Pits." As he turned to head back home I noticed that he only had one spur on, so I yelled,

"Hey do you know that you only have one Spur". He just laughed and said,

"I figger if I can get one side moving the other side will follow."

We were moving up past the Nelson farm and I kept yelling at Diane to go further ahead and watch the driveway. She rode back and said, "there's a bunch of drunks up there behind the caraganas yelling and partying, and I'm not going there."

I said, "you'll have to or the herd will be all over their yard and garden." She reluctantly went ahead and waited at the gate. Out staggers this very drunk man with a beer bottle in his hand saying, "Shay who are you and what are you doing out so late?" He didn't say early because they had obviously been partying all night.

Diane replayed, "I am Lorne Maull's wife, and I am trying to keep the cows out of your yard."

To which he said, "I know that old coyote. You're a pretty good looking young chick. You didn't have to marry him did you?"

She responded, "certainly not. How could you think such a thing?"

After a brief pause he got a look of surprise on his face, drew back a couple more swigs from his bottle of beer and stammered, "I'll bet you could use some help. Hold my beer and I'll saddle up the best damn horse in the district and give you a hand?"

Diane told him, "you might need that drink to get your horse saddled." Back he staggered behind the caraganas to the loud party, and forgot about helping. Thank goodness!

Things moved along quite well. Jessie was pushing the calves, and I was keeping the cows moving. Jessie would never bite a calf. He would watch the cows carefully, and when they had their weight on a back leg so they couldn't kick, he would nail them.

I am not sure what happened next but I think that Jessie came out of the tall grass in the ditch and spooked Charlie Brown, the big gelding that I was leading. I was walking and switching the poky calves. All I remember was feeling the horse's chest on my back, and one big black hoof appearing on each side of my head, and then the bridle bit smashing down on my head.

I woke up lying on the gravel road with my hat scrunched over my ears, glasses bent, and a lot of blood and gravel in my face. I still had the reins in my hand. Charlie Brown was standing looking at me as if to say,

"Sorry boss."

Jessie was still calmly working the herd. I slowly felt all the parts of my body to see if they worked. I decided that God didn't have room for me in his bunkhouse that day, or else just wanted me to finish the job. I thought of that stupid saying, "Cowboy Up," which I hate. In the rodeo arena there is always medical help available.

Out on the trail you just get up on your feet and say, "Please God, you pick them up, and I'll put them down."

When we finally got to the park gate and the rest saw me Diane was worried, but Randy just laughed and said, "So that old horse finally got enough ambition to dump you?"

I said, "No. I don't know what really happened, and I guess that Charlie Brown and Jessie will never tell."

Sorting with Necklace & the dogs

CHAPTER 21
MOVING CATTLE

It was July 1st and there was always kind of an unwritten law amongst the ranchers in the area that you turned out your breeding bulls that day. Don't ask me why, but in the earlier days if you didn't have your bulls out by then your management abilities were frowned upon. One bull was given out to every 25 cows, now that's a pretty lucky fellow I would say.

We had a neighbor who was getting married on July 1st, and took his bulls out in the morning. On the way home his old truck broke down. He had to jump his horse out of the horse trailer and ride ten miles back home, ending up a half hour late for his own wedding. He took a lot of kidding over that one, but the marriage has lasted fifty years, so I guess there was no permanent harm done.

Not only did the men know it was time to get the bulls out, some of the bulls did too. We had one huge big white bull about 2600 pounds called Huggy Bear. When he heard the stock trailer rattle into the bull pasture he would come moaning softly across the pasture and if the trailer door was open, he would step right into the trailer, and look around, as if to say, "Let's go boys I'm ready."

On this particular day we were also moving 75 head of cows across Highway 13 to fresh grass. One of our men and a good friend was helping me, along with my two working dogs Jessie and Aussie Blue. I was riding my big quick mare Molly. She was well trained and as the old timers said, "she could turn on a dime, and give you 6 cents change." Randy was riding a big red stallion that he was breaking for a bucking horse contractor. Rusty had sired some of the best bucking broncs, and the owner wanted him "broke to ride". Randy did this as a sideline to make a bit of extra money. Randy had spent a lot of time on him, and Rusty was coming along really well. In fact he hadn't bucked Randy off in the last three days.

Between the dogs and us we had rounded up the cows and calves and were pushing them toward the highway. There was a lot of bush and some of the calves had to be roused from their beds and didn't want to move, so there was a lot of yelling and swearing to keep them moving.

Did you know if a cow tells her calf to lie down in one spot, it would lie there for hours and not move, until sometimes hunger would drive it to find something to suck? I have found them lying all scrunched down and they would not move even an ear. Other times they would leap up, run in a huge circle sometimes up to a half a mile radius, and come back and lie down again in the exact same spot.

Better disciplined than some kids we have all known.

Everything was going fine crossing the highway until one calf saw the white line on the pavement. His mom hadn't found him yet, and when he saw the white line on the highway he quit the herd and headed back to where he had come from, as fast as his four legs could carry him. I quickly shut the gate and we took off after him. Molly was in hot pursuit because she thought we were on a roping mission and the dogs thought this was great fun. Both were well trained but in the heat of the chase no one was listening, or stopping. We raced the calf about half a mile through trees and hummocks then finally got him turned back. You couldn't throw a rope because the horses were running flat out and jumping deadfall, and if you took a swing with the rope and snagged a tree branch, things could get very ugly.

I looked directly ahead and there was the water hole, and I knew it was fifteen feet deep. The calf with the dogs on it's heels hit the water wide open, and all three disappeared. About fifteen feet in, up pops the calf and the dogs right behind swimming like mad. I made a quick circle and when the calf beached on the other side I threw a rope on him. He was pretty tired and wet, so Randy jumped off and lifted him up to me on Molly and he got to ride across that dreaded white line.

We watched the herd awhile to see that everybody had mothered up, let the bulls out, and were ready to head home. I just happened to remember there was one more gate to close, but Randy said, "I'll ride back and do it as Rusty's not tired."

He goes cantering back at a pretty good pace. He was about a quarter mile from me when down goes Rusty's head and he starts bucking. He must have had a flashback to his old Rodeo days and about throwing a cowboy into the dust of an arena, instead of the cowboy swaggering up to the pay window.

I wonder if he could hear the crowds cheering as he bucked higher and higher? Randy lasted about five jumps and went head first into the grass.

There was no movement and I thought, "Oh God here comes Hospital City." I jumped on Molly and went racing back to see if he was alive or not.

We were nearly there, when out of the grass staggers Randy. His old cowboy hat scrunched down over his ears, blood running out of his nose, a big scratch on his face, and tears running down his cheeks. Molly saw him about the same time as I did and she did a U turn.

That day her turn on a dime gave me at least eight and a half cents change! With one hand on the saddle horn, a spur hooked into the cantle, and the other hand on the ground I had a gopher's eye view of the grass conditions in that pasture. I managed to stay with her and get back into the middle. I got Molly stopped and went back to check on the fallen cowboy. He was sitting up rolling a smoke, and managed a feeble grin.

We rested awhile, rode back to the trailer, loaded the horses and headed for home, another uneventful day in ranch life.

Moving Yearlings to Pasture

CHAPTER 22
CALVES IN THE HOUSE

In the early days your only corral was your lariat. People didn't have "Vets" to take their calving problems to, or if they did they likely didn't have the money to take them. Many "manual deliveries" were made by saddle horse and lariat, small tractor, or several men on a rope. Often calves had to be "turned," and occasional stitching up was required. Every neighborhood had someone that was good at deliveries. When a farmer ran into difficulty calving these men would always go to help, and of course have a visit and a friendly cup of coffee afterwards. Since the advent of the calf puller and the maternity pen, one or two men can accomplish much more efficient and safer results.

Many a newborn calf owes its survival to being carried half frozen to the house, being placed on the old oven door, and getting a gunny sack rub down to get the circulation going. Sometimes a little spirits were poured down its throat. The ears and tail were often frozen stiff, and of course eventually would fall off, the "tell tail" sign of an early calf.

When we were first married we calved out our cows in February and March and had many experiences with cold babies. Earlier calves meant bigger calves to sell in the fall, which meant more dollars in your pocket. I would make maternity rounds on a regular basis night and day. Our old barn would only hold a few calves and mamas, so if it were full or the weather severely, cold the calves came to the house for a warm up. All going well, after a newspaper rub down, and the night in, they were away to their mothers. Of course, one always finds the odd heifer that won't take her calf, and has to be tied up to be taught maternal instincts.

The entry in our old house could hold up to five calves and sometimes did. Extremely chilled calves –those whose mouths were already cold were usually given a warm bath in our bath tub, to thaw them out. Ice crystals could sometimes be seen forming on feet, ears, and nose, when you first put them into the water. After a rub down they'd be put under an electric blanket to dry off.

We have over the years become a firm believer in "Bill Sidey's" remedy for weak or cold calves. A couple of raw eggs, well cracked, and poked down the calf's throat shell and all, was usually a high protein kick start to life.

One year we had an extremely bad scour problem. Until the vet's found that it was not ordinary scours, and developed a vaccine from our herd to combat it, we had great problems. There were days when I rode and roped calves nearly all daylight hours, popping a couple boluses down each suspect, or sick calf's throat.

We had let the cows spread out, to lesson the chances of infection on 13 quarters of land. It was most time consuming, but after a couple of months it certainly improved my roping skills, and "Lucky," my saddle horse became a well-trained rope horse.

If the sick calf did not respond to the boluses and became dehydrated, we then had to drench them with a hose and tube on a pop bottle full of warm water, containing one teaspoon of soda, and one half teaspoon of salt several times a day. If they didn't come out of it quickly they had to go to the vet clinic for several days of I.V. Electrolyte Therapy.

The lucky ones lived and were able to come home again. Before you could put the calf back on the cow you needed to have it's mother milked out, or it would become sick again, because the scour bugs thrived on milk.

Our herd became the basis of a study of the Guelph Veterinary College, which produced the vaccine "Scour Guard," which saved many baby calves in the cattle industry.

When we moved into our new home, a neighbor was appalled at the thought that I might bring baby calves into it. She was politely (I hope) told that it was the baby calves that were paying for the house.

It was during the first spring in the new house when on one of my midnight rounds, I found a baby calf, which I believed was premature and nearly dead. Being an optimist, I brought it into the house anyway, and put it in the utility room. I returned to bed and told my wife that I thought the calf was well on it's way to the big pasture in the sky, and that I shouldn't of even bothered with it.

A couple of hours later, I herd something banging around. I got up to check. The next thing my wife heard was a great flow of profanity coming from the living room.

The still wet newborn calf had come alive and had wandered into the living room, fallen several times on the rug, leaving yellow blotches, then deposited a large amount of manure, lay down in it and ground it well into the rug. I thought that we'd never get it out, but lots of soap, hot water and elbow grease left the rug spotless again, by 4 a.m..

A friend of mine tells the story of when she was young, part of a large family experiencing hard times. A baby calf had been orphaned, so had been taken into the house. Upon the unexpected arrival of an upper class neighbor, the proud mother rushed the calf and her children into the bedroom with strict instructions. Every time the calf started to move or to bawl, they were to sing loudly to drown out the sound, so the visitor would not know that there was an animal in the house. To the children in the bedroom, the long-winded lady's visit seemed endless.

Lucky

Chapter 23
Calving

Calving season was just about over, and things had gone pretty well.

You know what I mean; the odd dead cow, and a few dead calves.

I always said any rancher that says he has a 100% calf crop and no trouble during the calving season is an out and out liar, or has a guardian angel in his hip pocket right beside his snuff can and jack knife.

Your saddle bag equipment changed as the season progressed from the calving chains and hooks to the modern medicines for doctoring, such as Pen. G, Vitamin A, Selenium and the most important item "Watkin's Camphor Salve." It was used for everything from chapped lips to hemorrhoids, to wire cuts and saddle sores.

Now after about two weeks of it rattling around in the saddle bag, nobody used to ask for seconds for their chapped lips, because they never really knew what it had been used on last.

Don, a young man who loved ranch life was riding with me through the hills checking the babies and their mama's, along with our two dogs. It was nearing the middle of May, and there had been lots of rain, so the grass was really getting green and lush. This meant that some of the cows where producing more milk than a small calf could take. The cow's bag would swell up and get very sore and sunburned.

I say bags and tits because that's the way a rancher describes things.

If you said udder and teats you would probably be classified as a Dairy Man, and that would be quite insulting to a rancher.

You never know if you may have to defend your honor of wearing boots and chaps to some young fellow in coveralls and gum boots, and smelling of hibatane. Especially at some church function, if he was spiking his lemonade punch with a flask from deep within his baggy coveralls, this you know a ranch hand would never do.

As we rode along we spotted an old cow, who every time the poor little calf would put his cold nose up for a suck, his mama would nail him with her back foot and send the poor calf flying about 15 feet. She would then run over and give him a lick, and wonder why her baby was just staggering around.

I commanded the dogs to lie down and stay back, and said to Don,

"I'll take her head, and you heel her. We'll stretch her out on the ground and milk her dry." I got her head the first try, but Don missed. She made a big circle and came around behind me, and got the rope under my horses tail. Old Molly clamped her tail down on that rope, sort of like a grizzly on a salmon, and took to bucking. She humped up about five times. It must have been the weight of the cow that jerked the rope out from under Molly's tail.

By this time Don had gotten a second throw and had the cow by both back legs. Both horses did their job of stretching out the cow. My old Molly had done this many times, and would hold the rope taught while I'd get off to help a cow calf, or treat her.

I jumped off and started milking the cow out, then put the tit salve on the bag. Sometimes the baby calf would come up looking for a drink, so you'd push his head down and shove a tit into his mouth. That way he got a much needed drink, and that helped speed up the job.

At the end of this whole operation the trick was to be able to keep the cow just choked enough so that when you jerk your rope off her neck, she would be still too short of wind to get up and chase you down before you could get on your horse.

All was going right on schedule except, when I jerked the rope free and went to run back and mount up,

WHO was sitting right behind me wagging his tail, as if to say, "Can't I help," but man's best friend.

THINGS GOT PRETTY WESTERN!

But I am still alive to write this. Afterwards when I was safely sitting on top of Molly,

I could't help but wonder. ISN'T IT WONDERFUL HOW AN UNATHLETIC GUY LIKE ME COULD JUMP OVER A DOG, GET TANGLED UP IN A LASSO AND STILL MAKE A JUMP, AND GET ABOARD A SKITTISH HORSE...........

WITH 1400 POUNDS OF SLACKED BAG MAD COW SIX INCHES BEHIND ME BLOWING SNOT IN MY BACK POCKET?

God was good to this old rancher that morning, and I'll bet he had a good chuckle looking down on the commotion below.

CHAPTER 24
EARLY CALVES
PLANNING AHEAD

I have occasionally been asked why we calved in the rotten weather in March, and April. First of all, the end of March and the month of April are supposed to be nice, as that is the way Mother Nature has supposedly planned it. The grass is starting to grow, the pussy willows are budding, and the wild animals are having their young. However, like some humans Mother Nature can be very vicious. Maybe she had a fight with Father Nature and decided sometimes to take it out on the world, by having a howling blizzard the middle of April or into May.

We as Stockmen plan our calving season nine months ahead of time, and can only hope for the best, after we turn our Bulls out. You plan for the breeding and calving season that will work best for your place, depending on fieldwork, and other big jobs you have to accomplish. Not every Rancher has the same type of operation, so the times can very. We neighbored with a lot of people. In fact we had 120 miles of fence. If you had a bunch of your cows cycling, and your bulls weren't out, you can bet that sooner or later, somebody's bull would show up, and you would get a few early claves, and not know which ones. This happens even in the best of regulated human families too. Big surprise but you must make the best of it!

One spring we got a howling blizzard, and the main herd broke into the willows around the lake for shelter. When I was feeding, I noticed some tracks going south, so I took the ¾ ton truck, stock trailer, and horse out to follow them. I unloaded my horse Molly at the lake and rode along the deep track in the new snow. About a mile in, I found this cow standing over a half frozen calf. She was one of our wild mean cows and very possessive of her newborn, shaking her head at me and pawing the snowy ground, daring me to touch her calf.

It takes an awfully good, and patient saddle horse to let you drag up a limp half frozen baby calf, especially when the cow is bunting her in the stomach and legs. I didn't dare get off my horse to lift up the calf out of the deep snow. I managed to get a rope on it's back leg and drag it up in front of me on the saddle, and headed back to the truck. I didn't worry about the cow leaving the place were she had calved, as in her mind the calf is supposed to stay there. As long as her body produces milk and the scent is there, she will keep returning to find her calf. She will wander off for food and water, but keep retuning for the next 3 or 4 days. The same thing happens in the fall when you wean the calves. Once the cow dries up, her calf is forgotten. If the cow can't hear her calf bawling she will stop bawling for it sooner. Also not much milk is being manufactured after the summer in over, and her udder is not as painful. Natures way, right or wrong, that's the way it goes in the animal kingdom, wild or domesticated. The young must find their own way, once the mother's body starts the reproductive cycle all over again.

Meanwhile, by the time old Molly carried the cold freezing calf and I back to the truck through the deep snow, its ears nose and tail were frozen stiff, and it looked as though it likely would not survive.

I threw the calf in on the floor of the truck, started up the GMC and turned on the heater full blast. I decided that I should maybe take another look around the backside of the lake through the bush. Sure enough there was another freezing baby calf. I remember thinking;

"Oh yes and our calving season isn't supposed to start for another three weeks." So I had to go through the same procedure, with a mad cow, but this was nothing unusual as we always ear tagged the newborns of the snuffy cows by reaching down off of the horse. Molly and I then hauled another heavy baby the mile out to the truck.

About half way back I could hear a motor roaring, and thought, "boy the snow ploughs got here early this time." As I got closer I realized it was my ¾ ton "reved" right to the top. I dumped the calf off the horse and jerked open the truck door.

The calf had come alive and had his head wedged under the brake pedal, pressing the throttle right to the floor. The temperature gauge was right out of sight. I guess I panicked and instead of idling it down, I shut off the motor. The two plastic reserve tanks on each side of the radiator exploded like two bombs and blew antifreeze and steam out of every corner of the hood.

Here I was two miles from home and out of antifreeze. I just threw the second calf into the cab, loaded the horse and waited for the engine to cool, then started the truck and took off for home. I'd drive until the motor got hot, stop for maybe 20 minutes until it cooled down, and then start up and go again. Without fluid, your temperature gauge doesn't work, so it was by guess and by golly on the heat. However, I did make it home and was sure that the motor would be shot. After I got new plastic tanks I drove the truck and it didn't burn a drop of oil, and was in use for two years after that adventure.

The next day I took the calves back to where they had been born. It's quite different to carry a half frozen calf on a horse, than to have a live kicking one on your lap, while still controlling your horse. When I got back to the birthplace there was the mean old cow still trying to stand her ground. I literally dumped the calf off, then it wanted to follow the saddle horse as Molly seemed like a good mother image. After ducking and diving, Molly and I finally got away from the calf. The Mama cow spied the calf and charged in. She was about to kill it, when she smelled it, and realized that it was her baby. They went around and around in a circle, the cow trying to lick the calf, and the calf trying to suck her. Eventually the calf got a grip and started nursing. This cow and calf were bonded right then and there.

The calves survived, both loosing their frozen ears, and tails, but those parts didn't weigh much anyway.

This just shows that no matter how you plan ahead, things sometimes can get out of hand. Whoever said that life is boring, never lived at our place!

Molly

◯

CHAPTER 25

THE INTERNATIONAL SITUATION
ON THE OLD 7M - RANCH

Don't get this wrong now, as it wasn't government or religious issues. It's just that we had our own Canadian International Ranch hands. One was an English fellow by private treaty, another English fellow who had been with us for three years, a New Zealand, and an English girl from the International Agricultural Exchange Association. There was also a former trainee's mother and father from Sweden visiting us. He was a veterinarian at home, or a "wet" as they say. He was so anxious to help us out.

We only had about 100 calves and cows to process that day, so with all this good help it should have been a snap. Don had just got a new saddle horse as Dusty, his old Arab, was continually leaving him on foot, bucking him off about every other day. The day before Don had gotten off to treat a calf and Dusty broke free and ran about a mile across the field. Don just walked over to catch him but Dusty, the sly old Devil raced back and stood where Don had dismounted him. After this mile and a half walk Don decided that it was time for a new horse.

He got this brand new black gelding that was supposed to be the best horse in Alberta, according to the seller. Don on his new horse, and the New Zealand girl were galloping out to help round up the cattle when all of a sudden down goes the horses head. He is in a serious bucking mode and off goes Don. It wouldn't have been so bad but Don lost his glasses, and he was very near-sighted. I am sure that if the saddle wasn't creaking, and his horse puffing, that he wouldn't of even found it. He and Annie spent the better part of an hour searching in the tall prairie wool for his glasses. He did find them unbroken and carefully climbed back on his "well-broke" horse and helped with the roundup.

The Swedish vet proved to be quite a wonder. Every time that he would stick the needle into a cow she would jump and break the syringe, and he'd shoot the vaccine all over the cow and us. So after wasting the vaccine and finding the broken needle in the cow and getting it out we were wasting quite a bit of time. I suggested that maybe he should take his wife off on a nice prairie ride, which he did. I don't know what happened on this ride and maybe I shouldn't know but they made it home just before supper time, holding hands on horseback and looking very romantic.

Andy, the Englishman on private treaty, was over here apparently because his Dad wanted him to learn about Agriculture. He was a good boy but under the false impression that England was our Mother Country. His mom and dad had been married in Westminister Abby. He and his sister were not allowed to eat with them as children.

He had arrived during calving season, and as usual, things were pretty raw and hectic. We were riding up through what we called the East Coulee and it was a beautiful place with the Saskatoon bushes in bloom, and all the flowers coming out. Andy said, "boy in England you would have to pay for a ride like his". I just said, "Andy we can darn sure arrange that."

We found a cow that just had a dead calf, so I put my rope on it and dragged it the 1 ½ miles home across the pasture. A cow will follow her dead calf for miles on the end of a rope, as she is accustomed to it's smell.

I had bought extra calves earlier because you knew that there would be still births and other troubles.

When we got home, I gave my knife to Andy and told him to skin out the calf and tie the hide on one of the spare calves. After about twenty minutes there was no Andy so I ambled up to the house to see if Diane had seen him. There sat Diane laughing so hard that the tears were streaming down her cheeks.

Apparently Andy had come roaring into the house, went straight down the hall to the bathroom, and was yelling,

"Come Quick, Come Quick, I cut myself."

She went flying down the hall and there was Andy with pants and shorts down to his ankles, turned around trying to lift his bum up to see in the mirror how bad the cut was.

He's saying, "How bad is it? How bad is it? Will I need Stitches? Is there a lot of blood ? Will I need a tetanus shot?"

Diane took a look and said, "It's O.K. Andy. It is barely a little nick, plus you would have had to have a tetanus shot before you came to Canada."

"What if I die from this?" he moaned.

She responded, "Oh we'll just pull you over the hill with the other deads."

In a disgusted tone he said,

"You bloody unreactive Canadians," and stalked out.

He turned out to be a great guy but had quite a few experiences here. On one of his weekends off he and two other young fellows got "drunked up" and entered a rodeo...bareback riding event to be exact. The day of the rodeo, when they were up, nobody would admit to being a coward, so they all crawled aboard their broncs. The first two just quickly bucked off and weren't hurt. However, Andy came off headfirst and ended up with amnesia. No one knew who he was. The other fellows went back home and went to work. Andy was in the hospital for three days and didn't know who he was or where he was. All he knew was that he had to get back to work. We didn't know where he was or what had happened.

When he got back to our house he just sat down at the kitchen table and said, "you're not going to believe this."

We had International Agricultural Exchange trainees for 23 years, and enjoyed including them in our family activities for the summer that they were with us. We visited many throughout the world, and have had some come back to visit us.

They came to learn Agriculture in Canada, but we learned a lot from them as well.

One year Brower came to us from Denmark. He was the strongest and gentlest fellow you could ever meet, but he had one vice. He loved to hunt and to fish. With his first paycheck he bought a gun. The first shot he tried the gun recoiled and the scope split his eye -brow, and he needed 12 stitches to close the gap. Talk about a black eye.

His goal was to take home to Denmark, hides from everything from a mouse to a coyote. This he did. He would skin them out and put the hides in Diane's deep freeze in preparation to taking them back to his homeland in the fall. They were all packed individually in plastic, and believe it or not he actually got them all through customs. One day he came into the house and announced in his broken English that he had shot at a coyote, but had lost the shell in the bush. He didn't know how to say that he had missed his shot.

That same year we also had a Danish girl helping in the house. Our family was going to a wedding, so the two Danes were going to hold down the fort while we went out for the day. Diane and I arrived home about midnight and as soon as we got out of the car we could smell skunk. Our walkway was about 100 feet long and the closer we got to the back door the stronger the smell got. When we walked down the hallway to our bedroom the smell was sickening. Annette the Danish girl came out of her room to tell us that Brower had shot a skunk, and of course picked it up and was as proud as could be about another hide. First he went up to the other hired mans house who was also an avid hunter, to show off his prize. The man opened the door took one whiff and yelled, "get the Hell out of here with that stinking thing!"

Next Brower went down to our house to show and tell Annette. She took one look and said, "get rid of that animal first, then take off all your clothes before you come into the house and go directly into the shower." He didn't want to get undressed on the deck.

She finally said, "O.K. I'll go into the kitchen, and close my eyes."

He was so modest and still thought that she might peek, and he did take off his clothes, but left his shorts still on. The laundry hamper was just outside the bathroom door, next to our bedroom door. Brower got safely into the bathroom and then reached out the door, and dumped his underwear into the hamper. It reeked skunk scent, as well as everything in the hamper. It took days to get the house aired out, and back to normal. The hide had ended up in the deep freeze but he had numerous layers of plastic around it.

Needless to say, Brower was not on the "best" list for awhile. Now we know why they use skunk oil in ladies perfumes, because it certainly does cling.

Ride' em cowboy

CHAPTER 26
LONGHORN BULLS

All the beef producers were looking for a way to improve their calving death loss percentage without the stress of checking your heifer pens every 2 to 3 hours, plus having to make those 4 a.m. trips to the veterinary clinic to have C-sections performed.

Somebody came up with the idea of crossing your beef heifers with a longhorn bull so that your calves would be much smaller. The saying was that, "using Longhorn bulls was like drinking decaffeinated coffee. They let you stay calm, and sleep nights."

So being fairly enterprising and a bit lazy, we hooked onto the stock trailer and went down to Elkwater, Alberta to buy some Longhorn bulls for our heifers. I bought 2 two year old bulls and 3 yearlings. I didn't need five bulls but one went so cheap that I couldn't resist him.

After we got home I knew why he was cheap.

He was just plain ugly and a dirty gray color. One horn pointed straight up about 16 inches and the other hung down over his eye. We named him Pronghorn and he would charge anything that moved.

It was early June and still three weeks until they were to be turned out, with the heifers.

What to do with them was a problem because no ordinary barbwire fence would hold them.

Several times I chased them for miles getting them trailed back home. One time just at dusk Pronghorn hit a barbed wire fence on the dead run and went along the wire about two post lengths, with his horn hooked under the wire. The sparks just flew from his horn like it was made of flint. I never thought a horn could be that hard.

After a couple of sessions of chasing these guys, I decided to maybe calve a little early, and turned them all out with the heifers.

I had to because really, all we were doing was rounding up bulls and fixing fence. Sort of like following a Seismic crew for an oil company, only I wasn't getting paid.

We soon learned that when longhorns get two or three years old they become almost undomesticated, and very possessive of their herd. Things were fairly quiet for awhile because they were busy romancing.

I was checking the pasture early one morning and there was one bull missing. Spot was gone. He was a magnificent red and white beast with a huge spread of horns.

I rode into the neighbors pasture and sure enough, there he was trying to enlarge his own herd with some of theirs. Guess you'd call that heifer rustling. He saw me coming on horseback with my dog Aussie Blue and headed for the home herd. He jumped a three-wire fence like a deer and then ran into the bush and turned to watch me.

I said to Blue, "get him out of there." He tore into the trees on command, there was a great commotion in the bush and finally out pops Blue.

He sat down right beside my horse and looked up at me at me as if to say,

"You fool, don't you know there's a mean bull in there?"

After half an hour or more of our supervision Spot defiantly went back to his own herd.

Things were quiet again for a couple of weeks until Jake the Field Boss for the Hutterites drives into the yard. He had Toby sitting with him in the front seat and Shorty sitting on the truck deck perched on a five-gallon oil can.

Jake says with a bit of a smirk through his gray whiskers, and trying to act mad...

"Lorne, you just have to get that bull out of our pasture. He pretty near killed two of my boys."

So we loaded up two horses and headed out again. Arriving at their pasture, sure enough there was Pronghorn, this time with his stolen herd of about 15 Hutterite heifers. When we rode up he put his head down and charged our saddle horses, then would turn and stand in a bush pawing and bellowing. The horses were getting pretty spooky by this time, as they had taken their share of hits from mad mama cows during the calving season. Every time that Pronghorn would charge they would run.

You know trying to rope a mad bull over the back end of a running horse .....

It Just Doesn't Work!

After a couple hours of this circus we decided that we needed a plan B. I whipped into town and sweet-talked the vet. into lending me his tranquilizer gun. Back on the range while Don kept Pronghorn's attention, I slipped in behind him and shot him in the hip.

In about 10 minutes he was fast asleep lying in a heap.

The vet. had assured me that with that dose he would sleep about half an hour. We quickly bailed off our horses, and put our two lariats around the top of his horns, one going each side.

We knew if they were around his neck he would likely choke himself when he got snorty, and tried to escape, or to charge a horse. He was wide-awake in ten minutes and on the fight, but pretty help-less with the two ropes holding him on either side. If he charged one of us the other would jerk him back and vice versa.

We eventually got him stone-boated into the stock trailer and into the front compartment, so we could safely load our horses in the back one. As Don and the dogs got into the cab he said, "what now?" I just said, "Auction Market time for Pronghorn there's a sale today."

When we got to the Market, I told the yardman, "we've got a mean bull here boys, and don't let anybody get hurt." They opened the gates of the sale ring and the Auctioneer announced,

"We have a fast mean bull here so take a quick look as he runs through and do your bidding later."

They opened the scale gate and he went through on the dead run. That was the last I saw of Pronghorn on his way to the big pasture in the sky!

I knew that I hadn't herd the whole Hutterite story, so the next week when I met Toby on the road I said, "so what's with the Pronghorn story?"

Toby grins then proceeds, "Well, we see your bull out in our pasture so Jake says get a couple of sticks and we'll chase him out and save Lorne the trouble. We were about 100 feet from the truck and the damn bull charges. I'm pretty fast and manage to jump on the back deck of the truck, but Shorty tries to get in the back door of the crew cab.

Pronghorn hooked his horn under Shorty's suspender and lifted him right off the ground. The suspenders broke and snapped back hitting the bull in the face. Well I don't know whether the bull stopped when Shortly messed his pants, or when the suspender hit him in the nose.

That's why Shortly was sitting on the oil pail in the truck box because Jake wouldn't let him ride in the cab with us."

Now doesn't that just go to show you that God looks after his own.... no matter where you worship!

Chasing Old Pronghorn

CHAPTER 27
TRAIL RIDE

This story took place nearly 40 years ago when our children were young. Jay was seven and Jodi was five. The work was caught up on the ranch, and Diane's Uncle Neal had invited us up for a Trail Ride in the Rocky Mountains. There was a young fellow from Denmark working in the Provost area. He spent so much time with us that we started to call him Paul Maull. The trail ride was to actually last one month, but Jodi was to be a flower girl at a wedding in three weeks, so we decided to ride in with the group, leave a little early and come back out on our own. The morning that we were loading up the horses, kids, and dog, Paul just happened to come by and had some time off so we just loaded another horse on the three-ton Dodge cattle truck. Away we went 250 miles to Rocky Mountain House. We arrived at Uncle Neal's late in the evening, stabled our horses, had a big supper and went to bed. Nobody slept much as we were all excited about our new adventure, and I do mean adventure.

Uncle Neal had been buying horses all winter and whenever they were about "half broke" he'd sell them to some outfitter, then go and buy some more green broncs, some not even halter broken. We were all up early and ready to pack up and head out, we thought. At seven we began packing. There were 24 riders (including our two children) on their Shetland ponies Sandy and Dandy, as well as 17 packhorses.

We roped horses, dragged them out and blindfolded them, would then ear them down and tie up a back leg, so we could put on the packsaddle. We'd turn them loose and they would come apart bucking and squealing. If the packsaddle didn't shift they would settle down in the herd again in about ten minutes. To make matters even more difficult, Uncle Neal had purchased a new set of pack-saddles with leather latigo straps. When the horses would sweat, the leather latigos would stretch and shift back acting as a flank strap. As soon as this happened the horse would usually tear into bucking and storm right through the whole herd. We had one big brown gelding that never tamed down. Even after three weeks every morning we still had to tie up his back leg and blind fold him or else he would cow kick you or strike out at you with his front feet. In this process of packing I soon learned how to throw a good diamond hitch so the pack would never shift. The standard rule was that the eggs, the whiskey, and the musical instruments were to be packed on only the gentlest packhorses. We couldn't take a chance of them getting broken.

We finally pulled away from the staging area at three o'clock in the afternoon. We tied most of them halter shank to tail and it amazed me how soon they settled down and became good packhorses. Our first major river crossing was across the river just up from the Ram River Falls. Diane and I were both leading difficult packhorses. Jodi was riding by herself across the river when her pony started drifting towards the Ram Falls. Diane and I were shouting at her to ride away from the falls but with the roar of the falls, she couldn't hear us. Some way or another the little pony got his feet under him and scrambled up on the opposite bank, just above the falls. It was a bad scare for us. We found out later that Shetland ponies will just tip over and float like a barrel downstream.

We trailed for nearly two days and everybody was starting to relax and enjoy the scenery. Each evening we would unpack, set up camp, and make supper. Then we would settle down for some music and story telling.

One evening there was a great commotion amongst the horses. They all stampeded by the camp and headed back up the mountain trail. We think that either a bear or a mountain lion spooked them, because they broke chain hobbles and leather straps like wrapping string. They left on a full gallop in a panic state. Luckily our horses were prairie horses and just formed a tight little herd and stayed put. I grabbed a bridle and jumped on my saddle horse Lucky bare back and tried to catch the run a ways. In the chase we crossed the Ram River three times. I will never forget the sound of that many horses running and hitting the water at the full gallop. I gained on them pretty fast as Lucky never liked to be behind in any race. Ahead there looked like a place where I could pass them and get them stopped, or turned. All of a sudden I was out of trees, and pulled Lucky to a sliding stop. Immediately in front of us was a 50-foot cliff, straight down. I never thought much of it at the time, as I had to back track and try to catch the herd again but when I looked at it later it gave me quite a start.

It took about another mile until I was able to get in front and I was beating on the head of the lead horse trying to turn them into a circle. He was so scarred that it didn't even seem to register on him. The look of pure freight in his eyes was indescribable. Luckily the people at the staging area heard us coming and pulled some trucks and trailers across the trail and we were able to get the horses circling and finally stopped and under control. Some of the other men from our group had jumped on our horses and arrived in time to help trail the whole bunch back. Fortunately, it was moonlight as it was after midnight when we arrived back in camp, to our very worried families. I was tired and ticked off as Lucky had lost two of her shoes and developed a bog spavin. The rest of the trip I had to ride a "half broke" horse that I had brought along as a spare. Cricket was a big sorrel mare who became my main saddle horse later on in ranch work. However, on this trip she didn't know much yet. When we were above the tree line and on goat trails, where you could look hundreds of feet down the cliffs, she would decide to prance, rear up and act out. Poor Diane wondered many times if she would end up a widow before the trail ride was over.

This was very interesting territory, and I always wondered why God would allow a scrawny old spruce tree to grow on these wind swept rocks. That day we camped on a ledge where the wind didn't blow. You could look down on the valley where the ice was still caught in a bend of the river. I saddled up again and rode down with a bucket and got a pail of crystallized ice. The women made us all drinks out of tang crystals vodka and ice. I still remember Uncle Neal toasting everybody and saying, "Boy this is just like uptown."

Our kids were good riders for their age but the pesky Shetlands had no withers and occasionally going down steep hills, the saddles would just slip ahead and go over the neck, and over the horse's head the kid would go. One time Jodi's saddle went over Dandy's head and she was lying on the ground crying. I said, "Come on get up and get on again." She said "Dad I can't, that so and so horse is standing on my foot!"

One day we were caught in a heavy thunder and hail storm. The sky litterly opened up so we all had to don slickers and took shelter under some big spruce trees. That afternoon we were going to cross a little creek called Malag, and would camp there a couple of days. Then our family would have to go back to the staging area and head for home. Because of the rain, this little creek had turned into a raging flood from the storm. We each took a kid on our big horses and snubbed the Shetlands up tight and forded the creek. It was pretty scary for us prairie people as the water was up over the stirrups and really flowing quickly. Blue Dog bailed in and was swept down stream about a quarter of a mile swimming as hard as he could against the current trying to get to the other side. When he made it back up to where we were he was totally exhausted. Two days later when we left to start our journey out, that same little creek was no more than three feet wide, just meandering along over the rocks.

Our main objective was to cross over the Mountain Range on the Ironstone Pass and look down over Lake Louise. This couldn't happen as the pass was still drifted over with deep snow banks. You could not ride through it even in mid July. We carried on in a different direction and went along the Clear Water Lakes. They were beautiful at this time of year. Some of the group tried fishing but had no luck, as the pike would not take any kind of hook. There was so much food in the lake that the three and four foot fish would just slowly swim past the hook no matter what color it was or how you jigged it.

We were still treating hobble sores, bruises and chapped fetlocks. We would bath them in salt water then smear on bacon fat. This was a very good treatment for the horse, as it kept the wound soft.

Our family of four plus Blue Dog slept in one small tent. We had a cook tent and extra tarps to break cold winds. The first while, we would bury the fresh meat we had packed in river rock below the water level where we camped. The water was near freezing and this acted as good refrigeration. Later we lived on canned or salted meat and the other basic staples. When traveling, we had a good breakfast then would pack sandwiches for lunch, and cook supper when we finally camped. In that country there was always good fresh water to drink. We were basically exposed to the elements 24 hours a day. Of course everyone developed chapped lips. At the start our cousin Billy made the statement that he had packed sufficient preparation H. We all laughed. He just said, "you wait you'll be coming asking for it, and it had better be for your lips." He was right!

One of the little girls came down with the mumps and was so sick. She was a real trooper and never complained. She just kept riding her pony and tried to keep a happy face, and not spoil the ride.

However, all good things must end, so we split from the main group, and headed back via the Ranger River to the truck.

Nothing much happened on the way out except for one incident on a high pass well above the tree line. We were going around a sharp V curve on a crevice with a deep drop. I had the packhorses tied shank to tail. One made it around the curve, the next horse was slower, so the front one was trying to pull the back one over the deep crevice, and the back horse was pulling back. After a quick look, I jumped off, grabbed my knife, and cut the horses tail hair off. I couldn't reach the rope as it was in the middle of the crevice and both horses were fighting for their footing.

We had no rifle along, and did see bear tracks quite often. By the time we arrived back at the staging area we all breathed a big sigh of thankfulness. In three weeks we had only met one other group out in the Mountains. The Park Ranger told us that at five years, Jodi was the youngest rider to ride her own horse into the Banff National Park.

Trail Ride

Chapter 28
Flying Lessons & Lessons Of Life

One October day, I had been to town and there had been talk of a flying school going on, so I signed up Diane and myself to take it. I asked her when I got home if she wanted to go and she said, "sure." She was always a good sport no matter what hair-brained idea I came up with. Then I said, "but you will have to go first as it starts right away and I must finish the harvest."

Later I got to thinking, "what have I done now, as I could get really car sick and imagine what a little plane would be like."

Diane got her license with flying colors and we bought a 172 Cessna. She and a neighbor pilot did a lot of flying, so she became a very good pilot. Every chance we got we would go flying, slowly at first to become acclimatized to the air. When my turn came I was sure that I could do it. My instructor was a little short twerp with a big handle bar mustache, which he would stroke, and never say a word.

The first time we got into the little 150 he just said, "take her off."

I didn't have a clue. He barked, "rev her up, when she gets to 60 knots, pullback on the stick, lift the noose, and let her fly." Away we went.

My first impression was like, when as a kid you'd grab onto a calf's tail and go flying across the yard behind it totally out of control. On that very first trip up he put us into a spin and I was completely helpless and ignorant as to what to do.

Finally he pulled it out very simply by just stepping on the opposite rudder, and going into a dive to regain our airspeed. When we leveled off he just looked at me and I said,

"You do that again and you'll be cleaning bacon and egg off this dash."

Flying School class work was tough for me. I had been out of school a long time and had no study habits. You had to learn the flying alphabet.. A Alfa B Bravo C Charlie etc.. As an example, our plane was Charley Gulf Juliet Tango Zulu, which we always used when communicating with the radio tower on takeoffs and landings. We also had to learn to read latitude, longitude, true headings, magnetic headings, and maps as well as the types of clouds. Airways protocol… west fly at even numbers altitude, and east odd etc, the pilot needed oxygen at 12000 feet, but the passenger didn't. It seemed like I was at a grade two level in a grade 12 class. It was rather funny one lady that knew everything failed the test.

I was lucky when flying, as I only had to look at the gauges for altitude. My peripheral vision was good and I could land by feel and sight.

A logbook was given to us where you had to file your flight plan. You entered your departure date and time plus your destination and estimated time of arrival. You had to list all passengers. If you ever went missing or crashed, Search and Rescue could zero in on your ELT, or Emergency Landing Transmitter very quickly.

If the DOT had ever pulled my logbook they would have wondered who Aussie Blue was. He was my Blue Heeler Dog who logged many hours with me.

We had been up flying one day and I had a lot on my mind and wasn't concentrating on my lessons. When it came time to land, I bounced that little bird four times about fifty feet in the air each time. I don't know why it didn't fly apart. After getting control the instructor started to give me Hell. I fired back and told him where he could put his plane and to make sure that the prop didn't break when it hit the buttons on his back pockets. However, the next day I was back to try again. We didn't need air conditioning in the cockpit, as the temperature was certainly cool between us. Flying,

I realized, was like sitting on a rocking chair, you could rock like heck, but you weren't going anywhere. I then really bore down and got serious about learning and getting my pilot's license. It seemed to go a lot better after that. I was doing spins, stalls, and 180-degree turns, plus not landing like a wounded crow. The instructor even seemed pleased.

At ten hours of flying time, I came out on the tarmac and did my walk around inspection, this was a must before take off. The instructor was standing by the little 150 and said, "you take her up and practice." I don't know if he really thought that I was ready, or if it was an excuse to kill me off. I crawled into the cockpit, said a short prayer and took off.

You never realize that there are so many creaks and rattles in the plane until you are by yourself and in total control of your life.

Nobody is there to help you except maybe the good Lord sitting right seat with you. It was a once in a lifetime thrill to be soaring through the air as free as a bird on your first solo flight. When I was coming in on final to land, I looked up and saw a plane coming down to land in the opposite direction, straight at me. We had no idea that there was another plane in the area, as he hadn't radioed for clearance. All of a sudden the flying instructor was on the radio yelling at him. "Get the Hell out of here I have a student coming in on final." The other plane made a hard right over me and disappeared, then joined the circuit and followed the proper landing procedure.

My cousin asked me later what it was like to fly solo the first time. I replied, "It is truly amazing to think that I was in God's guarding hands, yet he gave me the freedom of being a human being and depending on man's knowledge to build a machine that would allow me to soar in space like one of his wild and free eagles."

I told him, "it's better than making love." He just laughed and said, "go on it can't be that good."

You needed 35 hours airtime and 35 hours book time before you were able to do your flight test and write the exam. I loved doing the short field take-offs where you hold the brakes and rev up the motor, then take your feet off the brakes and the plane would leap forward into the air like a turpintined cat.

I flew 150 miles to Wetaskawin to do my flight test and cross country test. The flight tester was a great big man about 250 pounds, and I was about 210. The DOT used a weight and balance weight for a man to be 160 pounds. I mentioned to him, "you know with just the two of us we are overloading the plane?"

He just laughed and said, "we have a long runway, take her up and lets see what you have learned." The flight test went very well, and I landed like a butterfly I might add. The flight tester crawled out and said, "now go and write your test and you will be a full-fledged pilot." I wrote the test and passed the first time, but soon realized that it was just a license to learn. With Diane now riding right seat we made many happy little trips about the country.

We had a half-mile airstrip at home that was dirt, but I kept it well groomed. I had trained on pavement and wanted to learn how to land on roads. The reason you learn this technique is in case of engine failure you need to pick a spot and are then committed to landing there. There is no second chance in a case like this. Here again you are in God's hands but you have to do your part too, like adjusting your air speed by pulling up the nose, and regulating your decent. In case of an emergency you just hope that you can mush it in without too mush damage to you and or the plane.

Pete, our crazy flying friend was more bird than man. He air sprayed and had been a flight instructor until the DOT had a difference of opinion over teaching his students how to survive in emergencies.

In other words, landing in fields and on roads was not in the flight manual.

Pete would do just about anything in a plane. He even put tire tracks on a combine cab once and almost caused the operator to have a heart attack. One day I was driving down the road in my new half ton on a clear sunny day with not a cloud in the sky. All of a sudden my truck box was full of water. Pete was getting ready to do some spraying and had sneaked up behind me in his Cessna 185 with a load of water. He dumped it all into my truck box and roared over about twelve feet above me, wiggled his wings at me and was gone. He thought it was a big joke.

I told Pete about wanting to do emergency road landing practices, so we went up for a flight and looked around. He was right seat and his little boy and dog were in the back. He spotted a road with gravel trucks hauling and said, "most of those trucks should be doing about 50 miles and hour, and there should be about a quarter of a mile between them. There are no power lines here so lets do some touch and goes."

More like hit and misses. I often wondered if a truck driver or two looked into his mirror and saw a plane right behind his gravel trailer. After doing a few successful touch and goes we went home and actually into hiding for a couple of weeks, because someone had reported us. The DOT was looking for a red and white plane but hadn't been able to get the registration number.

We had many good times with our little bird. Our Blue Healer Dog also loved it. He would sit right seat and when you landed at an airport he would get a lot of attention. He hated having to sit in the back seat when Diane came along. We all spent many happy hours of fun in the 172 checking cows, as well as checking neighbors. They had no secrets in those days, as you could look right down in their farmyards. We flew for quite a few years, but one day I had a blackout while pen checking in the feedlot. I woke up with about 200 heifers looking down at me. The doctors said no more flying until we find out what is the cause. It took about a year until finally they told me that I could pass a medical again.

One day another pilot neighbor phoned and asked if I wanted to fly with him to Calgary to go to the Bull Sale. So away we went. Upon reaching Calgary International Airport we were on final, with radio clearance to land. We were using 20-degree flaps and coming in smoothly. All of a sudden the tower dispatcher screams into the radio,

"Make a hard left and get out of here, there is a 747 right behind you." He gunned the motor turned left and there was the tower in front of us, and the 747 behind us. He skillfully got us out of the dispatchers screw up. At that time if you caused a big plane to re-circle there was a 250 dollar fine to be paid.

Flying home in the dark was another thrill for me as I didn't have a night endorsement yet, and this was my first night flight in a small plane. You are dependent solely on your instruments and dash lights. When we lifted off from Calgary it seemed that lights could be seen for hundreds of miles. You can have your landing lights on but until they have something to reflect off of you can see nothing.

This experience reminded me of religion. You think that you are in control of your life and there is nothing but space in front of you. At sometime in your life flight you must put on your landing lights and have them reflect off God...or else you are just flying through space and have no hope of ever seeing eternity, and landing safely in Heaven.

When you file your flight plan of life your departure date is unknown.

Your E.T.A or estimate time of arrival is also unknown to us....

But your destination should always be Heaven.

Our Plane J.T.Z.

CHAPTER 29
A BAD SITUATION AT CALVING TIME

It was a cold March morning and we had one small pasture with 100 cows due to calve. Ron came back for a second load of silage, and told me that some of the cows were acting a bit strange, so I drove out to have a look.

One cow was down, and I thought that it was bloat, so I stuck her to let the gas off. As I continued to walk through the herd, cows were falling over, and would chase anything that moved. I phoned the Vet. and he said, oh that's a sign of the times it's spring. Did you just get your fertilizer in?

I said, "yes a B Train was delivered late last night and that we had used the grain auger to unload it." He suggested that some of the fertilizer must of stuck in the grain auger and that when Ron had put it into the chop bin, that a small amount had broken loose, and then mixed in with the silage. It was 48-0-0, tastes like salt, and is very deadly to livestock, and it causes nitrate poisoning.

The cure was to give 100 cc of Printers Ink intravenously into the juggler vein, and drench each animal with 3 gallons of vinegar. The vet only had a small supply of printers ink on hand and he picked up extra vinegar and headed to our place. In the meantime Diane took off to the different towns that had a newspaper, and printers ink. She went to Consort, Lloydminster, and Sedgewick to get all the printers ink that they could spare, plus emptied the local grocery stores of all their vinegar supply.

In the meantime we were treating these crazy mad cows. Some were convulsing and down, so we had to hang them up by the neck, with a rope on the front-end loader. It was some job to find a juggler vein with the cow trembling and convulsing. Some how the vet would manage to get 100cc of the printers ink into the juggler, and then we would push a hose down her throat and pump down three gallons of vinegar.

Some of these cows had already calved and the vet did not know if the poison would go through to the milk and kill the calves as well. Fortunately it didn't. As Diane got back from each of her different directions with the ink, and vinegar, we would keep treating more sicks, and those that looked even remotely sick.

The first cow that went down, and I thought was bloat, died about two hours later. She had likely got the first bite of feed, and the strongest dose of nitrate, which only had to be a very tiny amount.

We had a new feed wagon that was excellent at mixing rations, so for the two-mile journey to the cows it was mixing the feed, and the tiny deposits of fertilizer throughout the load of feed.

One old cow was completely crazy, and jumped the fence and headed north. The vet said, "Let her go, we have enough to treat here." I don't know what happened to her but three days later she came back with a baby calf at her side, none the worse for the wear.

We treated everything that looked sick and then chased them into a small corral. Guess the cows that got the silage first were the sickest as some looked pretty good, but we treated everything that we could handle. By the end of it all we had about 80 of the uncalved cows in a small corral where there was a big poplar grove of trees, and of course some of the trees had fallen over, so it was pretty touchy trying to keep track of things. There was no power there for lights, so with a flashlight I was slipping from tree to tree, just to keep from getting charged by these mad cows.

Then the fun really started, most of these cows were heavy in calve and started giving birth. Out of the 80 cows 35 had calved by morning. When the mothering instinct kicked in or they turned to smell their new calf I didn't dare help them at all, as they were out to kill me. All I could do was watch and hope that none of the calves were crooked or had the skin over their nose. When these cows gave birth the water in their water bag, plus their urine was the same color as the printers ink.

This was a very stressful day and night, but of course with that many cows calving to close together, there was some confusion as to who owned what calf. It really didn't matter which cow raised what calf, as long as every calf had someone to suck, and to love it. That too took a few days, and a lot to patience and hard work to get sorted out.

I often wondered what happened to the truck driver who had delivered the fertilizer when he got back to his base. It was his first road trip with a heavy load. He loaded at Medicine Hat, and was supposed to head north to Metiskow, Alberta, but instead he went south and ended up somewhere in southern Montana, before someone got him turned around. He had to have crossed the border twice, both going and coming, and the border guards didn't even bother him.

He missed our road and came in from the north down a very steep slippery hill, with a 90 degree turn at the bottom. He must have been a good driver to be able to maneuver 48 tonnes of fertilizer in the mud, but he sure couldn't tell north from south. We unloaded him about midnight and I guess that's why a little fertilizer was stuck in the auger, as by then everyone was so tired.

It was just another episode in life that you live through, and continue on with the cow business.

CHAPTER 30
RANCH RAMBLINGS ERIC

As I write some of the life experiences that happened during our ranching career at Green Meadows Land and Cattle Company, or as we called it the 7M Running Bar, let your imagination overrule common sense, and come along with me for the ride.

It was a lazy Saturday afternoon that Mickey and I had ridden out to check the yearling pasture. She was a German Trainee, on our ranch for the summer and loved working cattle with me. It was the normal routine check for pinkeye, foot rot or anything unusual. She was all excited this day because her mother, sister Martene, and brother-in-law Verner were coming to Canada, and were due to arrive at our place.

I was a little apprehensive, as I had just hired a new hand by the name of Eric…. sight unseen. He too was supposed to be coming.

As we rode up to the calving corrals on the Bevan Place, in drives my wife with Mickey's family, and behind them comes Eric….all 350 pounds of him. Introductions were made. I was still sitting on my big brown gelding Chewy.

Eric came over and started fiddling with the bridle. He said, "you know I was quite a rider in my day. Do you mind if I try him?" to which I replied, "I don't mind if you think you can handle it."

I dismounted.

Eric quickly came over, sticks his foot in the stirrup and proceeded to reef himself up.

Chewy looked around and saw this heavy weight.

I knew something was going to happen!

Eric was just about up in the saddle and his right leg came down heavily on Chewy's rump.

Well the horse just blew up, and tore into bucking.

Eric bounced about 4 or 5 times on the saddle horn with his big tummy. With every jump, you could hardly see the top of the saddle, and the horn was completely disappearing into his midsection. A couple more lounges and he ended up crashing down into the corral fence.

I caught up Chewy and walked back to where Eric was lying gasping on the ground.

I'm not usually stumped for words, but all I could think of to say was, "it's a good thing you didn't break the fence or you'd know what your first job would be tomorrow."

Not a smile came from the group watching. Mikey's Mom's eyes were as big as saucers. I'm sure that she was wondering what her daughter was doing in this Wild West. No one said a word.

Eric got into his truck and headed back to the main ranch. Mikey and her reunited family got in the car with Diane and took off across country as well.

I loaded the horses and followed in the truck and horse trailer.

About a half mile ahead I saw the car stop to open the gate. It didn't move, so I wondered if they had trouble. Upon pulling up beside them, I saw that they were all leaning on the car hood convulsing in gales of laughter.

Verner, in his broad German accent saying,

"Du Big Yelly Belly bouncing on dat hoss." The tears were streaming down his face.

I said, "shame on you all for laughing at poor Eric," and doubled over the steering wheel and was as helpless with laughter as they were.

Home Again

CHAPTER 31
ERIC AND THE HEIFER

It was a brisk November morning and a lot of the pressure was off. The combining was done, the calves were weaned and we had two big pits full of silage. The bad news was that we had the feedlot full of freshly weaned bawling calves, and an outbreak of pneumonia had become a challenge. With acute pneumonia you had to treat them very early or they would die. Most times even after aggressive treatment they might die or sometimes remain a chronic case. This meant that they would keep eating but wouldn't gain weight, usually succumbing to some other ailment before the winter was through.

Either way it was a bad deal.

Our saddle horses had just been shod with corks in their shoes so that they could move quickly and safely on the frozen ground and icy patches. Alvin and I were cutting real deep in the pen that morning for a second wave of pneumonia when we spotted a bad case.

Between the two of us and my border collie Jessie, we got her up into the barnyard. The next move was to get her as quietly as possible into the treating chute. With pneumonia and a high fever the animals can get real crazy. They will charge anything that they see and then fall down. After they get their wind back again, they will stagger up and look around for the next moving object to charge. This heifer really went on the fight. She was a big black baldy and about 800 pounds. We left the horses outside the yard for safety sake, and tried the Mexican Matador trick waving our jackets at her, then when she would charge, we'd jump up onto the corrals fence slowly working her toward the treating alley.

While we were in the process of doing this, in drives Eric with the silage truck. I had him out feeding the range cows thinking that he couldn't do too much damage there....I guess other than running over a cow or two. He watched awhile, then crawled over the fence and strides right into the middle of the corral. He plants his fat stubby legs apart and holds up his fists like the great John L. Sullivan and says, "try it you S.O.B." Eric still weighs in at about 375 pound with his baggy gray sweatpants and tee shirt that did't quite meet in the middle. There was about five inches of hairy belly showing and it made an excellent target for the heifer.

She aimed for him and came hurtling across the corral wide open. When her head hit his stomach, it totally disappeared. You could have sworn someone had cut her head off half way up her neck. They both went down in a heap. She then tried to get up and get her footing, but Eric was so round that she rolled him about three times before she got all four feet gathered under her, and was getting ready for another charge.

In the meantime, Eric is up and heading for the safety of the tack room, his little short legs were churning like the spokes on a buggy wheel pulled by some high stepping thoroughbreds. Just as he was about to round the corner to safety, she nailed him again in the left back cheek and he goes flying airborne. The good part of it was her momentum carried her on past him, and he was able to scramble to safety, into the tack room. I jumped down off the fence and ran over to check on him. There he lay on the floor gasping for air like some big beached Beluga whale. I said, "are you O.K.?" He looks up as he gasps, "that's not in my job description."

I looked across at Alvin. He was doubled over laughing and managed to say. "that's the best unrehearsed rodeo act I've ever seen."

It's a good thing we had our laugh then because the next time the heifer charged across the corral she crashed into the fence and dropped dead. I guess her lungs exploded. Alvin said "I'll get the tractor and drag her over the hill."

But I said, "No you had best check on Eric first…you may have to make two trips over the hill."

I went back to pen checking, as it had to be finished before dark. That evening when I met Alvin, I asked about Eric. He told me that he had helped him cripple back to the house, and his wife insisted that Alvin help him get into the bathtub. Well you put that much man in a bathtub…. there isn't very much room for water. After the soak, then Alvin had to help Eric's wife reef him out of the tub, and get him into bed. He laid there for three days, and then limped down and gave me his notice. He had decided that he was a little out of shape and that ranch life was just a little to strenuous.

Jessie at work

CHAPTER 32
DAVID & THE THREE LITTLE PIGS

Many people believe that ranching is just like you see on T.V. I'll tell you folks, "that's not the way it plays out."

Our Ranch was a fair way from town, and not many people lived anywhere near us.

If you saw dust coming down the road it was either;

A friend
A bill collector
A salesman
Or the R.C.M.P.

And believe me, we saw them all at one time or another!

David came to our Ranch looking for work early one spring. He desperately wanted to be a cowboy. He wore a pair of those little goofy glasses, and a big felt cowboy hat. He came in an old beat up ½ ton truck with two cute little girls hanging out of each window.

I thought, "now here is a man that wants a job and is trying to support his family." I had trained lots of green hired men before, and they turned out well, so I gave him a chance with a job.

He was able to catch on to doing some things, but other things he just couldn't seem to get the hang of. Teaching him was rather like trying to pour five gallons of water into a one-gallon bucket.

We had just finished up the fieldwork and usually every year Grandma and Grandpa and ourselves would go on a fishing trip for a few days. We left David in charge to just check the place daily to see that everything was in order. If he had time, he was to go up to the north field with the big White tractor and bring back the breaking disc, so we could start working some oil well sites when I returned.

David was going across 200 acres of summer fallow with nothing to block his view, but he managed to hit a 7000 Volt high line power pole with the tractor, right between the front wheel and the grill. When the pole hit the front axel of the tractor it snapped like a toothpick. The electric wire came down and whipped the two top lights off the tractor cab. He was not hurt because the power breakers up line switched off. It was a long weekend so most of the Calgary Power men were off duty at the various community sports days and picnics.

Whoever was on call went back to work and just switched on the power source for the main line again, and then went back to what he was doing. The only problem was that this line on our place was now hanging about four feet off the ground fully charged.

One of our cows came along and touched it with her wet nose, was flung in the air and landed right on top of the wires. Needless to say, she was fried pretty quickly and tripped the power off again. The power crews were called back to go and look for the problem.

When I arrived home, I was pretty mad at the power company for turning on the power without knowing where, or what the problem was. If it had been a person on a bike, or any other creature had run into the live wire they would have been toasted. I was told that if they turn on a breaker and it works and stays on .. end of case, "We assume all is fine."

I then said, "what about my cow?" I was told that they wanted $3,000. for the pole, and maybe we should just call it even. I had to fix the tractor, had lost a cow, and then had to find her calf and teach it to drink from a bottle. Some more summer jobs, that I didn't need or want.

Towards the end of summer we had brought in a bunch of first and second calf heifers to feed them grain. I have always believed that you had to look after them extra well the first couple years, and then they had to look after me. We weaned off their calves and put the heifers in a separate corral where they would be given extra grain, or chop as we call it.

David's wife asked if she could keep three little pigs and buy the feed from me. I said yes, and told her that she could have the feed for nothing, as we wasted more in any given day than her pigs would eat.

Two weeks later David phoned and said that a bunch of the heifers were acting funny, so I drove over to the other place to have a look.

When I drove into the yard I knew immediately what was wrong. It was rumen overload!

This happens when a cow eats too much grain and her stomach stops working, and the grain starts to ferment. They bloat up and it is just like alcohol poisoning. They simply lie down and die unless you can get them up, get them moving around, and their stomach working again.

David's wife had gotten feed for her pigs and left the chop bin door wide open. There were still heifers at the chop bin door fighting to get in and get chop.

I phoned the vet clinic, and they said, "bring up as many as you can get to move." We sorted off about 20 and tried to get them loaded on the three-ton trucks. They staggered like a bunch of drunks, but we were able to get most of them loaded.

One died trying to get up the loading chute, and another was dead in the truck when we got to Wainwright Vet Clinic 45 miles away. Then the work started. You pushed a big hose down the cow's throat, followed by a small garden hose down inside it. You then filled the cows belly with water until it was tight as a drum. You pulled out the small water hose and started kneading the stomach with your arms and legs. This irrigating system forced the chop out. It took about 2 hours of repeating this process on each cow, until you got the grain out of the stomach. There were 3 to 4 five-gallon pails of grain in each cow.

There was no guarantee that it would work. If it did, sometimes the cow would die later, as a result of the stomach lining sloughing off from all the trauma. We worked all night and finally got the last one done. One cow died at the vet clinic and two more died at home.

The next day I went over to look at the disaster and David and his wife came out. He did feel badly about it all, but then his wife said, "Does this mean that we will have to pay for our pig feed now?"

I looked at her, then at the sky and quietly said, "please God give me the strength not to commit murder."

I thought of the two little girls and knew that they still needed a mother.

A week later David came to me and said, "I guess this isn't the life for me" and gave me two weeks notice. I felt like jumping into the air and yelling hurrah, but realized that every man has a certain amount of pride, and I didn't want to lower his self esteem any further.

On the spot, I paid him for two weeks work and told him that he could leave anytime that it was convenient for his family. In two days they loaded up all their belongings and the three ten thousand dollar pigs, and I never saw them again.

We could have brooded over this happening forever if we choose to. But yesterday is gone and done, and you must forgive and forget if possible.

Tomorrow is always a new day, so just saddle up and ride into a new sunrise, and hope that God has a better workday lined up for you.

Our cows swath grazing

Chapter 33
Our New Truck

It was a great day and a special event on the 7M Running Bar Ranch. We had purchased a new four-wheel drive ¾ tone truck. It was lime green and had a four-speed manual shift transmission. It had enough power to pull the old fully loaded stock trailer anywhere you wanted to go.

I always said that the person who invented the four-wheel drive and the impact wrench certainly deserved a place in heaven.

Being a guy that needed a lot of equipment in my business, I immediately put a gun rack on the back window. You would hang your 30 30 Rifle on the top hooks just in case a coyote should get smart with a baby calf, then you had your lariat, a stock whip, several ball caps and a place for your Stetson. On the dash you had your tally book for baby calves and a can of snuff. I didn't chew but it looked good anyway. There was an assortment of pencils, ear tags and markers, some of which would end up in the defroster opening just when you needed them.

In the back I made a toolbox that had a complete set of tools, and also my Old Blue Heeler could ride on top of it. From there he could look down on the cows and be Boss Dog.

My wife wouldn't drive the truck to town because she said that it looked like a cross between an ice cream truck and a creation from the Red Green Show.

Also, I forgot to mention that I welded a big bracket on the front bumper, where the spare tire was mounted. If you remember, the tire was always bolted under the box. If you had a flat tire the spare holder was usually all rusted up and you had to lie in the mud or dirt and try to unlock the blamed thing. All the local ranchers of the day seemed to have mounted their tire on the front of the new trucks. Some of the mountings were really fancy chrome, but mine was constructed out of old well casing and painted black. A real beauty to behold!

One beautiful spring evening Diane and I were driving out through the calving pasture, of course she was opening and shutting the gates. We were putting along in low gear and the four-wheeled drive was engaged.

I spotted a cow stretched out and having real labor pains. Upon closer inspection we could only see only one front hoof and the nose showing. Diane said, "let's go back and get the horse to catch her, to get the calf straightened." With only a little daylight left, I knew that it would be pitch dark soon. I wasn't the best roper in the world in broad daylight, let alone darkness.

So I said, "you drive the truck and sneak up on her, as quietly as possible. I'll stand in the back of the truck and rope her and dally on the new tire rack."

We snuck up really close. I swung the rope twice, and let fly... missing her. The old fool jumped up like I had hit her with a whip, and took off on the dead run.

Diane says, "Now what?"

I said, "no problem. I'll sit on the hood, brace my feet on my new spare tire holder, and you drive after her." She was a little cautious, and I had to keep hollering,

"Faster honey faster...keep up to her."

What a T.V. Commercial for a GMC truck...

Me on the hood.....

Old Blue Dog on the Toolbox.

Most times when you rope off a horse you throw down and it is fairly easy to drop the rope over their head. Sitting on the hood of a fast moving truck, when you swing your loop and throw, it sails out like a frisbee, and wouldn't drop over the cow's head. After quite a few wild throws, and sharp turns I managed to get her around the neck. I took a quick hard dally on my spare tire rack, yelling.

"Stop! Stop! I Got Her!"

I didn't realize just how quickly the new truck could dig in and stop. I came off the hood like I had been shot out of a slingshot. I must have done about four summersaults, but luckily ended upright on my feet. I looked back up just in time to see my old Blue Heeler come off the toolbox like a Russian thistle ripped out of the ground by a sixty mile an hour wind. He was rolling towards me and I didn't want him to scare the cow, so as he rolled by I yelled

"Heel."

When he got his footing he took one look at me, disobeyed a direct command, and headed for the ranch on the dead run. I thought, "boy he needs some more basic training in obedience."

As my head cleared I took stock of the situation. My brand new spare tire frame and carrier was ripped off. Luckily the front tire of the truck was sitting on it. The old cow had been flipped on her back and was lying there out of wind. I grabbed the calving chains, then pushed the baby calf back in, straightened the leg and pulled it out, then dragged it around in front of her. As soon as she smelled it the old mothering instinct kicked in, and she started mooing and licking it, daring anything to come near her baby. .

I undid the dally off the spare tire carrier frame and had Diane back off it. I threw it into the truck box as I said to Diane.

"I'm a little out of wind, would you mind getting my new $40 rope off that old cow?"

She said, "No you Stupid Idiot get in the truck so I can get you home and cleaned up and see if you have any broken bones."

So I slumped into the passenger side of the truck thinking. "boy is she sensitive today.....I wonder if she had a bad day in the kitchen?"

On the way home, I remembered that I hadn't checked to see if it was a bull or a heifer calf, but it didn't matter because all my pencils and tally book along with everything else were all scattered around the truck cab. It was still bothering me about not getting my $40 rope off that cow!

AND THEN I PASSED OUT.

The Boss and the Foreman

CHAPTER 34
CHRISTMAS POEM —
ITEME

I started to write this story down, but just couldn't get my head around it. Diane suggested that we put it to rhyme.

As ranchers we are really shepherds, or the keepers of God's creatures. Most times I believe that we do a pretty good job of it.

Every Christmas our saddle horses and dogs, would always receive a little extra ration of feed. We have had many wonderful Christmases. However, there was the odd one that wasn't so good, and we wondered if God had taken the day off, just like the hired men.

This is a story of a very bad and expensive Christmas and an outbreak of a disease called Iteme.

Many a time on Christmas Day
I've fed the cattle and put out the hay.
It seems that I was always the one
To let the hired men have the fun.
They all had children who needed them there
So give them days off. That's only fair.
We had all pitched in and fed up ahead,
Strawed everything down with a fresh new bed.
All the treating was done, not a sick to be seen.
The feed bunks were full, and all was serene.
The day before Christmas arrived clear and kind,

We'd all have time to relax and unwind.
Grandma and Grandpa came up for the night,
To be in on Christmas and all it's delight.
My last trip through the feedlot on Christmas Eve
There was a strange critter...I could hardly believe.
He staggered around as if he was drunk,
He even tried to crash the old feed bunk.
I phoned the Vet. to see what to do.
It's Sleeper... Iteme you'll have very few.
One or two a pen is all you'll have to treat,
60c.c. of longpen, you'll have her beat!
By the light of the moon I went to treat that Critter.
I thought I heard Santa's reindeer patter and pitter.
Christmas morn dawned early clear and cold.
Of course the kids were first out of the fold.
Opening gifts... a family time of joy.
But there was work to be done for this young
cowboy.
As soon as dawn broke it was time to go see
How the feedlot servived the minus 35 degree.
First pen I checked three down and four deads.
Second third and forth ..seemed they all needed
meds.
Back to the house I go in distress.
"I'm going to need help to deal with this mess".
My wife and I dressed as warm as we could,
Left Grandma and Grandpa in charge of kids,
Christmas and food.
We carried the unconscious on the frontend loader,
Into the barn and a little more shelter.
It's hard keeping penicillin from freezing at minus
thirty five.
In fact it's hard for a cowboy just to stay alive.
We treated, and treated, and treated some more.
We could't keep up to even the score,
Of the sick and the dying, plus feeding the herd.

This Christmas had turned into One Big Barnyard
Turd!
Broken needles, frozen fingers and toes,
Chilblains and fogged glasses only added to the
woes.

The tractor and loader were busy hauling in and out,
This was no mild... Iteme bout.
A new disease with no prevention or cure,
We had a real disaster going for sure.
My wife joked this loader's the ambulance of the 7 M
Bar
With service like this we'll soon have them on par.
But as the day wore on things only got worse.
The tractor and loader became the 7 M Hearse.
At dark we rolled in for our Christmas feasts,
Had a brief visit..then back to sick beasts.
So on it went for most of the night,
We ended up treating everything in sight.
400 head.... a penicillin shot from the Boss,
It's the only way we could minimize the loss.
It took us three days, this team of husband and wife,
Cold hard work treating those... still clinging to life.
Some got better, the others quit getting sick.
We finally saw daylight, but not very quick.
We were worn out, tired, and mentally depressed.
We had missed all the joy. Christmas had passed.
And so it goes in this ranching life,
You always depend on your family and wife.

Moving cattle home

Chapter 35
Ranch Ramblings P.T.

It's back to a Ranch Story again. Don't let fear and common sense stop you from climbing into an old parka coat, and putting on your winter boots, if you don't mind working like a fool for a day.

It was a cold November morning and we were going to preg-test our herd of cows. I had booked the Vet. to come at 10 a.m. that morning.

If you don't know what preg. checking is, it's when a Veterinarian puts on a long plastic glove with petroleum jelly on it and shoves it up a cow's rectum, usually up to his shoulder. He then can either feel the fetus, or the blood veins feeding the unborn baby calf.

The only problem that morning, was that I had a late night phone call the night before from the meat packer. They would give me a premium price for two loads of fat heifers if I could have them delivered to them by 2p.m. for the afternoon kill. This plant was in Red Deer, which was a good three and a half hour drive with a Cattle Liner.

I liked about 200 head in a fattening pen because that made it much easier to check for sicks. Each Cattle Liner would hold about 45 head so we had to sort out the best 90. These heifers were big Char- cross, very athletic, and weighed about 1200 pounds each.

At daybreak we were running these heifers down the alley, through the narrow spot where two men were on two different gates. As each heifer went by me I would yell Catch or Bye. Catch meant the Catch Gate would open and the animal would go to the catch pen to be shipped. Bye meant that the animal was still too light and would go into the Bye gate and back to the fattening pen.

Things were going very nicely, when I heard an agonizing scream, and turned around. There was my English hired man rolling in the snow and the cattle streaming by him, on both sides. With his winter parka and wooly gloves he was writhing around on the ground, and clutching himself, like a giant caterpillar that had just gotten a shot of Raid.

Like Gramma, who would never say a wrong word, would have said.

"She got him quite high, up front, low down".

One of the heifers had leaped into the air and kicked sideways, and got him.

His wife came flying over to get him, and rushed him to the hospital. The rest of us had to finish loading the heifers, then get the cows in, and get ready for the Vet. coming.

The walking wounded arrived home about then and informed me that nothing was broken, but that some of his equipment was bent pretty badly, and that he should put an ice pack on it for a few days. He headed for his house, and walked pretty bow legged, like a real western cowboy who had spent his life in the saddle.

There was little chance for sympathy as we had 300 or 400 cows to Preg. check, and we were now short a man to help.

In drives the Vet. I knew him well, and he was always crabby.

Sorta like----if your dog had a disposition like he did you would shoot him.

We started running the cows down the alley into the chute as fast as we could. Of course Dr P. was his usual grouchy self and was barking out orders, "Close the Gate.. Fasten the Squeeze. Close the gate faster, squeeze the cow tighter, and on and on."

To this day I don't know how the guys did it, but somebody managed to shove a big rangy steer into the lineup. Well the Vet. rams his arm in up to his shoulders, and gets the funniest look on his face. He pulled out his arm and looked at his fingers, and wiggled them, then does the same procedure again. Then he lifts up the steers tail and has a look, and bursts out laughing.

That seemed to break the ice, and we all worked and laughed, and got the job done.

After the long day was done we were all sitting around the supper table laughing and talking about the days events.

Drinking some pretty strong "coffee" of course. Diane had phoned her Dad to jump in one of the Cattle Tucks heading to Red Deer to get the cattle weights and the cheque from the packing plant.

To make a long story short he and one of the cattle drivers had picked up a bottle on the way home and they were fairly happy upon arrival home. He walked into the room and in a loud voice says,

" Well boys we got rid of the Old Nut Cracker today!"

Chapter 36
"Peter"

Most times on the ranch, when the sun is shining, and everything seems in order it looks like a good time to saddle up your horse, and go for a ride. I knew that I'd be out in the Wainwright Military Park all day checking cattle so Diane packed a lunch for me, and of course a sandwich and some smarty cookies for Jessie. Off we went like carefree boys out of school.

It didn't take long for things to change at home, and Diane had to make some pretty major decisions. The gas man phoned and told her that there was a price war on with fuel 3 cents a liter for diesel, and 5 cents for purple gas. It had to be ordered by 2p.m. that day. She went back over her farm book records and realized that we had been spending $ 20,000 per year on fuel. She ordered $ 15,000 worth of fuel, and figured that it would last us for two years.

We had to get some big grain bins to store all the fuel, and it lasted for three years, this kind of showed us that somebody was cheating a bit on fuel delivered.

The day after the big fuel purchase there was a farm sale up at Andrew, Alberta. Some fuel tanks were for sale, and I also needed a fertilizer spreader that was offered for sale. Andrew is over 180 miles north of home so a friend of mine and I jumped into the ¾ ton, and headed out again leaving Diane as boss on the spread.

As soon as we got there we went and got a cup of coffee, and were sitting drinking it on an old wagon. Where we were was a very rural old Ukrainian settlement. Two older fellows who were sitting behind us came over. One had noticed my cap with the name Metiskow on it. In broken English he said,

"Metiskow…where de Hell is dat place?" I explained.

He continued, "I hear they had big fuel war down there too. Did you buy some? You know up here some of the guys bought up to 350 gallons."

They sat down behind us, and began visiting amongst themselves. One fellow says to the other one. "So how is your shoulder Steve?"

Steve says, "Not good. I still go see chiropractor."

The other man says, "Steve I hear big court case coming. What happened anyway?"

Steve tells his story, "well Peter buy this big tractor… you know kind…8 great big tires, and air conditioner. This morning it wouldn't start… and Peter has to go to town, so he phones the mechanic to come and fix."

By the time the mechanic comes, Peter has gone to town. I tell mechanic, "Peter thinks it's the alternator."

The mechanic puts on booster cables and away goes big tractor!

I run along side and try to jump up into cab, but the God Damn big wheel lug catches me and throws me to ground. That's why I am still seeing chiropractor.

Anyways, tractor knocks front off mobile home, hits holiday trailer and crushes the manure spreader.

When I finally get into the cab, I have to back that big son of a bitch out of the basement."

Mechanic says, "I guess it was alternator."

I say, "You get the hell out of here, or Peter will make alternator out of you!

Anyway now big court case…. Peter suing $30,000 for the house, $20,000 for the motor home, $6,000 for manure spreader, and $1500 for the drill."

And I say, "but Peter it didn't even hit the drill."

Peter just says, "I don't give shit. I'm "sue-ink" him anyway."

CHAPTER 37
TEAM PENNING

When I started competing in Team Penning or Cattle Penning as some called it, it took place in a hockey arena. If a ranch had a good corral it could be held outdoors and was a great social gathering as well. Most Sunday afternoons people would gather to drink beer and bet on who had the best horses.

It took a lot of cattle. 30 head would be run in and numbered. Three of them would each have the same number from zero to nine. Three quarters of the way down the arena a small 10-foot square catch pen was made. There was a chalk line across the middle of the arena. When your three-man team rode across that line your number was called out. In that herd of 30, there were 3 cows with the same number on their back. The team's job was to cut out the three, get them down the arena, and into the pen within three minutes. If you had 2 or more cattle with the wrong number cross the white chalk line, you were automatically disqualified.

It was a lot of fun as some of the horses would take to bucking, or the cows might charge them. The crowds loved it as there always seemed to be something going on to stand up and yell about, or just let off steam after a couple of beers.

My old mare Molly just loved taking part, as she was so competitive. When you rode up to the start line the announcer would call, "Flags Up" and yell out your number, Molly would rear straight up and buck and plunge. The spectators loved her. I am not ashamed to say that I pulled leather many times just to stay on her. There is nothing more embarrassing than to be lying flat on your back, and the wind knocked out of you in the middle of an arena, with the crowd oh-ing and ah-ing…. you think that you can nonchalantly wave and get back on your horse? Sometimes yes you can, but most times no you can't. It sometimes took awhile of writhing around in the dirt to get your wind back.

Molly was used to bringing "sicks" out of the feedlot, and always hated to go back a second time. There was one rule that you couldn't be rough with the cattle or you would be disqualified. She thought nothing of slamming them into the boards, the whistle would blow, and that was the end of your run. However, if you did get your numbered cow out of the bunch she would never let up for a second until the animal was penned.

It used to be a lot of fun, but soon many people were buying very expensive cutting horses, and our old ranch horses just couldn't compete with them. With more expensive horses the entry fees went up, as did the prize money. Many guys would cross enter, sometimes several times, which became very expensive.

If you only entered once and got three runs, you might do a lot of sitting on your horse waiting for the next run. If you sat a good part of the evening your horse would cool down. When you made your run on a cold horse, you risked hurting her with pulled muscles etc. This could ruin your good steady ranch horse. Sometimes if the entry fee was reasonable ($40 or less) I would enter a couple of times. There was a Jack Pot.

This was still better than golf, as those with the best times did win the Jack Pot, and got a little money back.

If we just had to sit and wait, Molly would start flexing the bit with her lower lip and I would just know that someone, or something was going to get kicked.

We watched the Penning Show in Calgary this summer, and the athletic ability of the horses was superb. I'm sure that many of the penning horses ranged from $ 30,000 upwards.

If my reflexes would get faster I might give it another whirl. However, lately when entering, I felt more like a sponsor than a competitor. So for now, I will just sit, watch, enjoy, and maybe have another beer.

Necklace & I going Team Penning

CHAPTER 38
SQUINTY

Squinty was a little ugly gray bull calf that wasn't a natural born citizen on our ranch. He was a C- Section, very lucky to be alive, and to be able to have such a good bovine life, although very short compared to a human life.

Now to go back to the beginning of his life story. It started at a winter calf sale at the Provost Livestock Auction. I had purchased a couple hundred head of green grass heifers, to put out to pasture about mid May. After branding them and giving them all their medical vaccinations, they were ready to go out for a peaceful summer of grazing and gaining weight. Sometimes if the heifers gained a lot of weight quickly they might bag up as if they were in calf, and going to produce milk.

I rode the pasture frequently that summer and picked out a heifer that was definitely very pregnant, not just slightly. Being small and only a year old, I knew that we'd likely be in trouble when she started to deliver her baby. I was on Molly, my good cow horse, so I roped her and kind of stone boated her over to the stock trailer. (Meaning she had all four legs braced and wouldn't give an inch.) When we finally got to the stock trailer, about 1/4 mile away, I dallied up real close and hard. I then stepped off Molly, opened the trailer door and said, "Get In". She scrambled in with the heifer snubbed up tight behind. The heifer had no option. It was either follow or have your head parted from the rest of your body. I slammed the back door shut and crawled in the side door of the trailer and was able to get the rope off her, as by now she was choking pretty badly. With that done, Jessie and Blue Dog my dogs, and I jumped into the truck.

We stopped long enough to have a cup off coffee, Jessie and Blue ate their smarty cookies and we headed for home thinking,

"Boy, doesn't this ranching life ever get any easier? "The coffee calmed me down, and the cookies must of relaxed the dogs as they slept the twenty-mile trip going home to the ranch.

Upon arrival we unloaded the heifer into a small corral, where we could watch her and waited for her pregnancy to terminate.

At the time, I was the 4-H Beef Club leader and we had the Achievement Day Banquet all planned. I had all the trophies, and prizes and program lined up. Just before I left, I checked the heifer and sure enough her labor pains had started. This was about 6 o'clock, and I knew that we would be home by 10, so away we went, leaving her on her own for that time frame and hoping for the best. None of us enjoyed the banquet much and rushed home, as soon as possible.

When we arrived back at the ranch she was trying to give birth. I checked her and knew instantly that this just wasn't going to happen. I phoned Dr Leitch at the Veterinary Clinic in Wainwright and he said, "get her up here quickly and we'll be set up to do a C- Section when you get here. We loaded her up and headed out the 45 miles. Upon arrival, the vets went to work immediately shaving the hair and freezing her side. In twenty minutes we pulled this little ugly gray calf out of her left side. From being pressured in the birth canal for so long his tongue was swollen up badly and it looked like a long big blue banana. The side of his head was flattened in.

After having straw poked into his nostrils to irritate him, he started to breath. The heifer didn't have any milk, but he couldn't have sucked anyway. The clinic always had frozen colostrum on hand, so he was tubed and fed that. We took a gallon of this home, but still had to tube him. His tongue still stuck out about eight inches and became very dry and chapped. We had to put baby oil on his tongue every time we tubed him and then we would put a panty hose over his head, pull it up, and tie a knot on top of his head. We had to cut out eyeholes so he could see. This kept the tongue moist plus encouraged the tongue to eventually go back into his mouth.

He would look at you with his flattened head and kind of squint at you. Hence the name Squinty was given to him.

This routine went on for over a month until the swelling went down and he could finally suck from a bottle. He became such a pet and would lie on the lawn at the house or under any of the shrubs that would give him some shade. Many people would come and say,

"Do you know that you have a calf in your garden, or lying under your deck etc?" We'd just laugh and say, "Oh yes, that's just Squinty. "

As he grew we knew that he would have to be castrated. After this operation, he went and hid in the trees for two days, but finally forgave me and came out for his milk. One of our hired men took over the chore of feeding him milk, and Squinty eventually thought that Ron was his mother and didn't realize that he wasn't human. .

One day I brought in a load of bulls, and when they came off the trailer Squinty took one look, crashed the gate and stood looking at the queer beasts from between Ron's legs.

That winter Squinty had a special stall in the barn with lots of attention and became a well-grown yearling ready for grass the next summer. I took him out to the pasture and turned him loose. He ate a little grass, smelled a few of the other steer's noses. I thought that all was well and started to drive out. I looked in the rear view mirror and there was Squinty racing behind the trailer to catch us. I knew that I should just keep driving, but I didn't. I jumped out and opened the trailer door. He didn't even slow down, give one jump and was into the trailer and turned around to look at me right in the eye. I swear that he was saying, "Get me out of here!"

Back home again, Squinty wandered where he wanted and ate what he liked. He would still lie around on the lawn or on top of some of the shrubs. He never really did any harm except for the odd deposit of fertilizer on the sidewalk.

The next time I took him out was to use him as a Judas cow and have him lead a bunch of yearlings across a road. We parked the trailer across the road with the door open. We rode our horses back to round up the yearlings leaving Squinty grazing at the gate. The plan being to then open the gate when the rest arrived, and he would lead them across the road to the new pasture.

About an hour later we arrived back with the herd of yearlings, opened the gate to have Squinty lead them out the gate.... but he took one look at the trailer, ran across the road jumped in, and proceeded to walk around in it and make a terrible noise, like a big garbage truck unloading a blue box. The herd stampeded and headed back into their pasture.

We started all over again, and eventually got them rounded up and across the highway, with the help of the dogs while Squinty lay in the trailer calmly chewing his cud.

Come fall, Squinty would wander around the feedlots to the different pens and eat what he felt like, but would never get sick from overeating. He got to be such a nuisance for the men that drove the silage trucks, because he would lie in the middle of the narrow feed ally. No matter how they would blow the horn he would not move. They then would have to get out, to kick him out of the way. They would just put him into the gate of the nearest pen or he'd do the same thing all day. By evening when everything was supposed to be quiet, Squinty would start to bawl and bawl to get back out of the pen and back to his freedom. Eventually somebody would get tired of his noise and go and let him out again. Both hired men said that he was a pain in the rump, but neither one of them ever missed a chance to scratch him, or talk to him.

By the time Squinty became 1600 pounds we knew that his job in life had been completed and it was a sad day indeed when he walked up the chute into the cattle liner.

I am sure that most animal lovers have had the odd Squinty along the way to enrich their memories.

CHAPTER 39

BIG DADDYS OF THE PRAIRIES

We had stopped for a lunch at a small coffee shop when in comes a young fellow wearing a shaggy gray fur coat with rings and pins stuck in every corner of him. I'm sure that by the look of him there was a lot more hardware, in places that we could not see. What shocked me the most was this huge ring through his nose.

I really had to chuckle and whispered to Diane, "remember the number of herd bulls that had rings in their noses that looked just like that?"

It was mostly the dairy bulls that were ringed because of their terrible tempers. People would heat a fork tine red hot, and shove it through the nostril cartilage, making the hole and cauterizing it at the same time. The ring would then be inserted. The bulls were handled with a long stick, like a fork handle, about eight feet long with a hook on the end. You could catch the ring with the hook to lead and control the meanest bull with no danger to the handler. I couldn't help but wonder, if this young fellow standing in line for coffee was led around by the nose, and what the handler, be it a he or a she might look like. The nose is so terribly tender that neither man nor beast would fight you if you had a hook or maybe a finger in the ring.

The male gender of the bovine herd are a very necessary part of the ranching industry. Like if there were no male humans you would soon run out of people to buy socks, and neckties for on birthdays and at Christmas.

On our ranch bulls were turned out for 60 days, as this gives you two heat cycles per cow. This would in turn keep your calving season to a little over two months duration. As soon as their job was done you would go out with your saddle horse and dog to try to bring them home back into the bull pasture for the next ten months, where they had nothing to do except fight, eat and chew their cuds.

Bull round up was very hard and dangerous work, as some of our big Charolais bulls weighed well over one ton. If your rope loop was too large and came back over their shoulders it took an awfully strong horse to hold them. In later years the sales people at the Bull Sales would have them well halter broke, so when they felt the hard pull of your lariat they would sometimes give a little. But most times no.

If two of you were working together one would hold the bull snubbed up to their saddle horse, while the other would ride back and bring up the stock trailer. He would drive up in front of the ornery thing and swing open the trailer door. If your dog was working properly he would bite the heels hard and the bull would jump into the open trailer door thinking that it was a gate. You would then slam the trailer door fast and bingo, the big guy was ready for his ten months of grazing and fighting with his bull mates. Sounds simple but these fellows knew that they were leaving their harem and would fight you every step of the way. Before the era of stock trailers many bulls were just left out, and that is why you got out of season calves.

In our later years of ranching we would sometimes have up to forty bulls in a herd. When you brought them into the feed yard for the winter, just like people, they would have to fight to see who was the alpha bull. Corrals, gates, feeders, and the stock waterers meant nothing when a half dozen bulls got mad and started fighting. You had better stay out of their way too!

They seemed to know if the old boss bull was getting older and less agile. Then the whole herd would pile on him, and he could do nothing but run.

We had two bulls that just hated each other, and would fight for no reason, except maybe a wrong look, or one just stood to close to the other. One was a big long horn called Spot, and the other was a shorthorn. As I walked into the corral one day there was Spot standing half asleep beside the wooden fence. I had just walked by when there was the loudest crack and bang just behind me. I spun around, and there was Spot laying in a jumble of broken planks and one eight-inch post broken off at ground level. The big white bull had T boned old Spot dead center, who was by now groggily getting out of the mess of splintered corral fence. He decided to run instead of fight, or I would have been in the middle of it all. I just thought you rotten so and so.(I didn't exactly say it that way.)

Now this may not sound too bad, but I had to put a fire over the broken off post stump to take the frost out, so I could dig out the old post and replace it. This took all night, and I still had to haul a few metal corral panels to keep the rest of the bulls in.

I went to town the next day and had to buy a big corral post and eight 2x8x16foot planks at a cost of $100 plus my time, to repair that fight damage. It was less than a week later that they got in another go round and Spot got his big long horn under the white bulls jaw, and held him off the ground about four inches. The white bull's front feet were flailing, but he couldn't touch the ground and he was being choked to death. Luckily I was there with the whip, and stopped that disaster just in time.

You had to be very careful when you ran the bulls through the chute to treat or ear tag them. If they feel a tickle on the hair of their ear, they could throw their head so fast, and break your arm in an instant.

There were still other uses for these big hunks of hamburger. In the early days they were used as beasts of burden. Imagine twelve of these big boys pulling freight wagons. These were oxen and I believe that they were castrated at a young age to take the fight out of them. They were still called Bull Trains and came up to Canada from the States bringing heavy loads of supplies. They were driven with whips, curses and lots of snuff. The wheels were never greased and you could hear the wagons screeching and squealing, for miles across the prairies. The dust from those Bull Trains could be seen for miles on the horizon.

Over the years some of the more athletic bulls would end up in a rodeo arena. They used to ride just brahmas and sit in back of the hump. The trouble with them was that their hide was so loose that you couldn't get your bull rope really tight and the rope would slip sideways. Now, with all the cross breeding you are getting tremendous athletic ability from these bucking bull programs. A horse will never step on you if it can avoid you, but a bull would just as soon kill you as not. There is just so much strength in these big beasts.

The Stock Contractors used to have one especially bad bull in a herd, but now with the A.I. Program they can breed a whole string of the same mean type. They had one bull in Las Vegas called Bodacious or Yellow Whale. He became very smart and would bring his head up and smash the rider in the face. He would leap in the air and turn himself sideways, like a big whale. He was eventually banned from the rodeo arena, but what did they do? The owner bred 700 cows to him by A.I. So now we have any number of mean killer bulls in the rodeo circuit.

It is supposed to be the biggest buzz that you can have to slide down on top of 2000 pounds of mean muscle, and try to ride for eight seconds.

Not for me thank you, as I know how strong and mean they can be.

One year we had just got our crop seeded and calving was done, so we decided to have a sleep in. Early in the morning from outside our bedroom window, on our new lawn, we could hear a big commotion. It was sort of a lowing and bellowing. We looked out and there were about 20 of the big fellows trailing over the lawn, pawing big holes in the grass. One Hereford with horns had stopped and challenged a spruce tree to a fight. He literally beat the crap out of a very nice five-foot tree, and was walking around with the branches stuck in his horns...sort of like an Olympic Medal around his neck.

We rented some bulls from Bill Wilson of Erskine for nine years which really gave our herd a big lift in quality, plus we only had them for the breeding season, so didn't have to feed them for the ten months, or have to chase them around all the time. If one got sick or foot root we would do an exchange. When bulls get foot root they could still breed a cow, but would be sterile because of the high fever. They are just like humans again, as a sore foot doesn't stop the sex drive.

Renting these good quality bulls, which we could not of afforded to buy certainly paid off, with the kids in the 4-H club. They just about owned the club for 6 or 7 years, with their Champion Beef Calves. It was funny the first couple of years the neighbors would congratulate me on the good calves winning. Later, they would hardly talk to me, and I'm not a bragger either. Funny what jealously does!

After renting these bulls for so long Diane suggested that we raise our own bulls, as the calves were turning out so well. Each year at branding we would not castrate about 20 bull calves, and then at weaning time we would narrow the selection down to 3 or 4, and keep them as herd bulls. You couldn't paper the calves, but who cared as we ended up with 35 bulls that looked exactly alike, and had a good rate of gain. I was very proud of this herd of big white Charolais Bulls.

We used to have a neighbor that was very possessive of his grass. If a cow got in and ate one blade of his grass he would be over and complain as if it had eaten a quarter section of his hay. One day his big bull got in with our first calf heifers. He came over with his hat in hand and said that he couldn't get it out, and that he didn't have a horse. He asked if I would mind coming over and getting it back to his herd.

I said, "sure." That evening I went out with my horse, dog, and rope. This was one big piece of mad bologna, and every time I would get near him he would charge my horse. I got him the first throw but I didn't think that Molly could hold him so I rode a couple circles around a big poplar tree. The problem was that the bull kept circling until he was right up to the tree trunk, ran out of rope, and was choking to death. He was gasping his last breath so I jumped off and cut my rope, and I wasn't going to give him mouth to mouth either.

He did live.

I often wondered what this neighbor would have said if he had found his bull dead by a poplar tree, with rope burns around the bark of the tree trunk. This bull learned his lesson, and after he recovered Blue Dog herded him home.

I kept this story between Diane and myself for years, along with many other humorous and sad tales about these big majestic beasts that were a big part of our western history.

The end of Old Spotty

CHAPTER 40
MANDY

One cold winter morning while we were having breakfast the phone rang. It was Adams Ranch wanting to know if we had any 4-H kids that wanted a baby calf. They were empting a pen of fat heifers and had found a little newborn black heifer calf in the muck. It's mother was ready for market and no one wanted to bother with it. Besides, it's mother had no milk.

Our daughter Jodi immediately jumped up and said, "I'll take it".

It was a school day, so she went off on the school bus and I went down to get the baby calf. It was lying on the feedlot office floor, dirty and shivering cold. Things didn't look very promising for her, but I laid her on the floor of the half-ton, turned the heater on full blast and headed back to the ranch.

Luckily we had a heated tack room in the barn with hot and cold running water with a "Micky Mouse Sewer System". We spent about an hour washing and cleaning her up, so she started to look like a baby calf and not a muck ball.

We had a bag of Nursette, and when you mixed it with water it was as close to colostrum as you could get. We filled a pop bottle with the milk, put on the calf nipple and gave it to her. She took it very greedily and never looked back after that first drink of warm milk. Some of the baby calves have to be tubed and taught how to drink and to suck the bottle, but not her.

Jodi would feed her before school and after school and someone at home would feed her at noon. This was quite time consuming, as it would take about half an hour for her to empty the bottle.

The next step was to get her to drink from a pail. Their natural instinct is to reach up to grab a tit to suck. First you wet your fingers in the milk and get the calf to suck the milk off them. When you get them sucking you push their head down into the warm milk, keeping your fingers apart, so the calf sucks up the milk, then you gently take your fingers out of their mouth.

If the animal is hungry it may take two or three lessons before you can hang a pail on the wall, and it will do it's own feeding without help. As the animal gets older it is normal for an animal to put its head down to drink water.

Jodi also had a pup that spring called O.D. and named her calf Mandy. Every day when she got off the school bus she would feed the calf and then she, the calf and the pup would play for hours.

They would race around and you never knew who was chasing whom. After the playtime all three would lay down in a pile of straw and rest.

What a sight, a black calf, a blonde girl and a white dog, all nestling closely in a pile of clean straw. Then it was back to the stall, the doghouse, suppertime and homework. You didn't pay much attention to it at the time but later in life you think,

"What a pity that more kids can't have an experience like that with animals."

Mandy grew like a weed and always would wiggle and squirm when somebody took the time to scratch and pet her. She was now a yearling, and went out with the yearling herd to see if she would become a mother cow.

Jodi was sure that she would become a 4-H Champion because she was so cute, but cute doesn't count in show conformation. But as a yearling she was the hit of the show as everyone would come up and pet her and she just wiggled and enjoyed every minute of the attention.

Most cattle will forget you when you put them on green grass for the summer, but Mandy never became wild and was always glad for a little scratching no matter where you met her.

The following spring during calving time we had all just sat down to supper, when one of the men came in and announced,

"Mandy is starting to calf".

The table emptied and everybody rushed out to watch and to see if maybe she might need some help. After about half an hour Mandy gave birth to a little longhorn bull calf all by herself. The calf was up and sucking in 15 minutes. She was a good mother and not mean and would let anyone pet her baby. This time Jodi thought she had a Cow-calf champion to take to 4-H. She showed them, but of course long horn cattle were not considered "Beef Breeds" so she and Mandy didn't get the Red Ribbon for "their baby".

However, Mandy was again the center of attention in the barn. That tiny little brown and white bull calf with its brand new red halter was a real showstopper.

Mandy never did get very big, which was typical of the Aberdeen Angus Breed in those days. However she was a good producer and had a calf very year for 21 years. The strange part of that was, they were all bull calves except her last which was a heifer. Most range cows do not live to be more than 12 to 15 years old.

When we moved south of Calgary, we of course brought along Mandy. She loved all the green grass and having less competition from the big cattle herd.

One day when we were having a Horse Training Clinic in our big arena, Mandy came up to the door, and it was obvious she was going to calve. I mentioned to the Instructor that our cow was going to calf if anybody wanted to watch.

The whole clinic shut down.

In a matter of minutes, Mandy obliged by having her last calf.. a heifer right at the arena door.

There were about 25 people watching, many city folk that had never seen a calf being born. They could not believe that the new baby was up and sucking in 20 minutes. The clinic resumed, but many commented on how Mandy and her baby were the highlight of the day.

Mandy at 21 years old

Chapter 41
Clancy

Clancy was the running rogue of our countryside. You never knew were you would see him. He never walked or trotted, it was always a very fast gallop. With his shiny red body, and long feathered tail straight back like a banner, he was a sight to see.

When he ran like the wind his lips would be pulled back and he looked like he was wearing a big grin. Some people were afraid of him as his big shinny fangs always showed. They need not of worried, as Clancy didn't have a mean bone in his body.

I first met this big Irish setter when we were trailing a herd of cattle out to pasture. He kept racing in and around the herd creating havoc for us. It was a great game for him. When he happened to run too close to my saddle horse, I flipped a loop on him, and had him caught around the flanks.

Now what do you do with a 98 pound dog biting, kicking and yelping on the end of your lariat?

I eased him along like he was on a leash for a couple hundred yards and then got down and took off my rope and said, "now Clancy, you go home before I get mad at you!" So down the dirt road he went, and didn't seem to bear a grudge.

One time late at night my brother was trying to pull the hitch pin from a tractor and wagon. Back in those days the lights on the old tractors were not very good. Everyone used to say that you needed to light a candle to see them. My brother was down on his hands and knees. He looked up and there was a mouthful of shiny white teeth looking at him.

You guessed it.

There was Clancy sitting on his haunches about two feet away watching him.

Clancy didn't always make his owner proud and the odd time he certainly did embarrass him. There was a public meeting at their place, I think about Pasture Management. Everyone was sitting around on the grass drinking coffee and discussing the program. The main speaker had on a leather suede jacket, no doubt a very expensive one. Bob said later, "I could see Clancy sniffing the air and I knew what he was thinking, but I couldn't get to him in time."

The dog simply walked through the crowd, stopped at the man with the suede jacket, lifted his leg and peed right across the poor mans chest. He then walked nonchalantly away as if this happened everyday in his dog life.

The farm where Clancy lived was quite a social place and many parties and all night poker games were held there. One March night, one of these poker games was in full swing when a fish peddler happened by. He had an old half-ton truck with a dog box on the back full of frozen fish. He decided that maybe there was more money in poker than in selling fish, so he bid into the game. They played all night and had morning coffee. The peddler checked his load of fish and there was not a fish left in the truck. He came storming back and accused the farm owner of stealing his fish. The owner said, "you saw me, I never left my chair all night."

It was a fish mystery, but when the snow melted everybody knew what had happened. Somehow, Clancy had gotten the back of the truck open and had worked all night, and had buried fish in every snow bank on the farmstead.

Probably Clancy's most famous escapade was when he wrecked a neighbor's brand new crew cab. The fellow was a very hard drinker, but this morning it was early and he was stone sober. They had shoveled seed rye onto the truck and it had pretty well filled the truck box. He jumped out leaving the truck door open and went into the house for coffee. The driveway was a long down hill slope with a bit of a curve at the bottom. When they looked out the kitchen window there was the new truck gaining speed as it went down the driveway backwards. In the driver's seat sat Clancy. He had obviously knocked it out of gear or park when he jumped in.

The truck was going pretty fast when it did a hard left, hit a tree, and came to a sudden stop. The seed rye washed out over the cab, the box came ahead about six inches and the doors all flew open. The truck shuddered for a few seconds and out of this wreck jumped Clancy. He took off like a bolt of lightning. Nobody knew where or when he stopped running. But I'll bet that it was quite a long way before he dared to even look back.

The Truck Owner said, "I know it's early, but could I please have a stiff drink?"

CHAPTER 42
AUSSIE BLUE

In the seventies, a new bred of dogs entered the Agriculture Industry. The bred came from Australia and was half dingo. They were the best cattle dog available to the ranchers. You could not get a registered one, as both the Canadian and U.S. Kennel Clubs refused to recognize them as a breed. They became very popular, and in the ranching business, you were nothing unless you owned a Blue Heeler.

We saw an ad in the Western Producer Farm Paper that read, "Blue Heeler Pups for sale. From proven cattle handling parents. All shots. Ready to go!" The ad was from Maidstone Saskatchewan, about 100 miles away. One Sunday afternoon we drove to see this new litter of pups ready for a new home.

We picked out one little fellow that was snow white, with a few black spots. The white hair grows in blue by the time they are a year old. Of course, he became Aussie Blue. He was a good pup and the strength in his jaws already showed the dingo in him.

Suddenly he became very sick so we took him to the Vet., only to find that he apparently had not been given his puppy shots and had a very bad case of distemper. Doctor Leitch said, "we can't do anything for him. Just take him home and make him comfortable in his own surroundings. Very few survive and if they do, they usually end up with the shakes, lose the enamel on their teeth or have permanent lung damage."

My wife, a nurse wasn't about to give up that easily and set up a bed for him in the utility room. Every time that his fever would sky rocket up, she would give him baby aspirins. This went on for three weeks. During which time he became partially paralyzed in his back legs and convulsed. One night we heard him dragging himself up the hallway to our bedroom and we both thought, "this is the end," but is wasn't, it was really the beginning of a long interesting life for Aussie Blue. He started to eat again, gain weight, started to play and was a real lively pup.

One night I was lying on the chesterfield playing with him when all of a sudden he bared his fangs, gave a loud growl and came for me. I gave him a really hard slap and he whimpered for a while. After that he was my dog, and never left me. The Vet. could never get over how he had recovered from distemper and had none of the after effects usually associated with the disease.

The next winter I took him to Obedience Training. There were 35 dogs taking the obedience class from the Wainwright Field Trial Association. There were very expensive and high classed dogs in attendance. Some of the dog owners "looked down" on a cattle dog that wasn't even eligible for registration in the Kennel Association. We went Sunday afternoons most of the winter. When classes were done we would always stop at the little store and buy a treat, to be shared on the way home. During the week we would practice what he had learned. At the final trial, Aussie Blue was declared "Top Dog" and received a nice trophy.

From then on it was ranch work, which he so enjoyed. He was tough as nails. He could draw blood in one bite and was better than any electric prod to move stubborn cattle. If I worked alone with him in the ally ways, I would just say, "Bring another one down Blue" and he would, quietly and efficiently. If the hired men tried to give him orders he would just go and sit on the porch and look at the corral as if to say, "I'm not getting paid to work for you guys."

He didn't particularly care for kids but tolerated them. He had a bad habit of standing on the truck seat with his front legs on the down turned window. He would always snap at the tree branches if you were driving through bush. He would grab a branch and then forget to let go. I don't know how many times he was jerked out of the truck window, but always seemed to land unhurt. You would slam on the brakes and let him back in the cab, looking all embarrassed.

Aussie Blue had a real passion for flying. He sat right seat and had many happy flying hours with me. If he had to give up "his right seat" in his truck or plane to another passenger, you could really see the disapproval in his body language.

Aussie loved to hook a ride on anything from the motor bike, saddle horse, boat or the back of the truck. I guess that he loved the feel of freedom and the wind blowing in his face with his tongue sticking out.

Blue Dog absolutely hated Hutterites… I don't know if it was all their black clothes or if they had a different smell, but you could certainly tell if one was coming up our walk. He'd bark loudly and wouldn't hesitate to duck under the deck and heel them as they came up the step.

We had Aussie Blue for over ten years, and knew that sooner or later his time would come. By then he was on lasix to make him pee better, the same as Grampa. Grampa kept him supplied with these Diuretic pills for over a year.

Although they are sad times these things happen for the best. A car had driven into his yard and being boss dog, he ran out to check, was hit and killed instantly.

I took him to the highest hill on the ranch and buried him, so that even today he can look down over his domain. I missed him a great deal because after sharing sandwiches and drinking from the same cup many times in those years we became very close. Life goes on, and I knew that we needed another cattle dog on our ranch.

Aussie & and his Top Dog Trophy

CHAPTER 43
JESSIE

Jessie was one of those big lanky Border Collies that could follow a saddle horse all day long and never tire out. Aussie Blue was getting on in years and his health wasn't that good so we knew that another dog would be needed soon.

Our son Jay delivered a load of feed to a customer and came home with this collie pup in the truck. Jessie had been tied to an old swather in the heat of the day and Jay felt sorry for him, so bought him. He never did say what he paid for the dog, but I guessed there wasn't much money left over from the load of feed.

Jessie was a true herding and working dog. Some dogs are "sicum" dogs, born to chase, while others are born to herd. In the old days you were the alpha dog, and to the collie, their job was to bring the meat back to you.

If you have a young collie when you take him out, if he doesn't make eye contact, doesn't crouch down, and put his tail between his legs, he is not ready to train.

Jessie was not the traditional collie and would herd anything that moved, including the chickens, turkeys, and pigs around the yard. He was probably trying to herd the saddle horses when one kicked him and broke his shoulder.

We took him to the vet clinic but they said that it was too high a break, and that they couldn't cast it, but that maybe the Veterinary Collage in Saskatoon could put in a plate. They warned, "It could be expensive, eight to nine hundred dollars."

My wife Diane said, "I just made out paychecks for several hired men for that amount each. I like Jessie better. Lets fix the Dog!"

The next day was a Thursday, so the vet. filled Jessie full of pain killers and he sat on the front seat for the 200 mile trip to Saskatoon. He was pretty sore by the time we arrived, and whimpering a bit. Sunday morning the Clinic phoned and said. "Come and get your Dog he has a 3 ½ by 4 inch plate in his shoulder.

When we arrived at the Veterinary College, they brought out Jessie walking down the long hall on a leash. I said,

"How are you doing Jessie?"

He just wagged his tail at me and pulled me outside and he peed on a tree for about five minutes. He was so clean that he could not bring himself to pee in the building for the three days that he was there.

We bought a bucket of Kentucky Fried Chicken, and stopped outside Saskatoon to have a picnic with him before returning home.

The clinic had said to keep him quiet for at least three weeks. Now can you imagine trying to keep a big active dog quiet, when he is jumping in and out of the half-ton, chasing gophers and the odd coyote? The clinic did a wonderful job on Jessie as he was never lame, and even the coldest weather didn't affect him.

From then on Jessie became my partner and never left me, be it on saddle horse, half ton or motor bike. I attended several dog training schools, because I knew nothing about the language trainers used.

After trying some of these, we decided that Jessie worked best with go right, go left, lie down and easy Jess. He worked with these commands, plus his own common sense, which was uncanny for a dog.

Jessie could be sneaky sometimes too. Several times I was going to town and would look in the mirror, and there would be Jessie in the back. He'd jump in the back of the half-ton, and lie flat on the floor until he knew you were far enough down the road that you wouldn't turn back. One time he sneaked a ride into town with the hired man, and jumped out of the back while the man was in a store. To find him was a job, and took lots of driving around town.

He finally spotted Jessie going down a back alley peeing on every garbage can as he went, like he was signing his autograph, or leaving his phone number.

He was still pretty young when he came with us one day. We were trying to get a big herd of cows through a gate. They wouldn't go and we wondered what the problem was. One of the riders squeezed through the herd, and sure enough there was Jessie guarding that gate with his life, so that none of the cows could get by him on his "Stand of Duty" job. She picked him up and threw him into the cab of the ¾ ton. After the cows were all through and the gate shut, I looked in the truck cab, and you would swear that a bomb had gone off. In his excitement of not being able to help he had ripped the styrofoam off the entire dash and the door. We had a metal dash and doors on that old truck for the rest of its life. You sure could see the gauges easily after that though!

Jessie never had a mean bone in his body. Anyone could pet him, and he would never snap or bite at a child. He had a system worked out for chasing cows. He would never bite a calf however, when a poky cow had her weight on her back foot on the ground, and couldn't kick him, he would nail her. That way he could get her back in the bunch without getting hurt.

We would sometimes be out on the range in the Military Camp, or moving cattle all day, so Diane would always make sure that there was a sandwich, or two, and some smarty cookies for Jessie, in with our lunches.

One time we were emptying a pasture, and one old bush hugger and her calf would keep quitting the bunch, and head back into the trees. You just couldn't get between that cow and the trees to get her turned. It became quite a game. Every time that she'd see a saddle horse, she and her calf would make a mad dash for the bush and freedom.

One day I was able to sneak up behind her and rope the calf then dragged him into a small corral, in hope that with him bawling she would come out close to the corral. After two days of the calf bawling, I managed to get between the cow and the bush, and then Jessie took over. We were moving her down the fence line and she kept trying to jump, and to break through. All of a sudden without me saying a word Jessie was under the fence and bit her nose badly. With blood spurting from her nose she went down the fence line and into the corral as if she had been trained. Jessie just resumed his place behind her, and acted as if it say, "I've had enough of you for one day."

I used to swear quite a bit, quietly of course. If Jessie would not do something right I would always say,

"God damn it Jessie" in front of every command.

He loved to help me pen check for sicks in the feedlot with Molly, my saddle horse, who wore her new shoes with corks for the ice. We could always get a sick out without disturbing the rest of the pen to badly.

I swear that Jessie could even pick out sicks himself. If you had a pneumonia animal standing with it's head down, he would go and quietly stand beside it until you got there, as if to say, "don't forget this one!" Once the animal was out of the fat pen he would take it up the maze of ally ways, all by himself, to the treating chute.

One day Diane came out to video Jessie working in the pens. I said a few commands for him and he just looked at me as if I was stupid and didn't know anything. I tried it a couple more times ...... same thing.

Diane started laughing and then said, "OK. I'll turn the sound off so you can give the commands in your usual manner."

Then I just said "Jessie God damn it go left" and he was off like a shot.

He did know his commands and was worth six riders to me.

Jessie had a romantic side too, which we didn't realize. One of our neighbors that lived four miles away had a black female lab, pure bred of course. He had taken her to Edmonton to get her bred several times, for 200 bucks a pop, but no luck.

I don't know when Jessie slipped over to help out, because he was always sitting on the deck ready to work every morning. This female dog gave birth to eleven little black and white pups, and you didn't need DNA to tell who the father was.

One year it was a late fall, so we had trucked the calves home from a herd of about 100 head of cows. We weaned them and thought that we would trail the mother cows home on a nice warm winter day. The trouble was that it never did get warm, so we would daily go down to this pasture with a load of silage, and chop the water hole open for them to drink. This was 14 miles from home so it was very time consuming. The year before we had pulled ten drowned cows out of a water hole and I was pretty anxious to get the cows home and away from the danger of them slipping into the icy water.

The temperature dropped down to −35, so I decided, "this is it- they have to be moved home."

Our hired man took the feed truck and I took Jessie and a saddle horse in the ¾ ton and the stock trailer. The cows knew the sound of the feed truck and Jessie was out quickly and quietly, urging the poky ones into the herd. We got out onto the road and started for home. Jessie would not get back into the truck, as he knew what his job was. He nipped the heels of the slow ones and kept them out of the ditches, and the neighbor driveway approaches all the way home.

Believe it or not, I didn't have to unload my horse out of the trailer until we were turning into our gate. I took my horse into the barn, to feed and unsaddle her. In came Jessie with icicles 4 or 5 inches long hanging from his jaws. His eyebrows were snowy white with frost.

Now you show me a human being that has that kind of dedication to do that much work, for a pat on the head, a good meal, and a warm bed.

We were always told that if you get nine years from a Border Collie that you are very lucky. We had Jessie for 21 years. He worked hard all his years on earth, and loved his job.

If there is a Doggie Heaven, I'll bet that he is still herding, and that St. Peter will have to say "Jessie God Damn it go left."

Jessie

CHAPTER 44

BLACK PRINCE

We were riding out in a yearling pasture when I noticed a sick animal that needed treating. I undid my rope and gave the horse that I was riding a kick and we took off after it. The problem was that my horses back leg slipped in the sand and she threw out her stifle joint. This is something like an athlete pulling a groin muscle. It takes a long time to heal and sometimes in animals it just doesn't.

It so happened that the next day there was the "Elite Horse Sale" in Lloydminster, so we took the stock trailer and away we went. In life I have learned that horse traders are about as honest as Jessie James and have just about as many scruples…..which are none.

Our neighbor had bought a horse at an earlier sale. The next day he attempted to saddle it. That old pony threw his saddle so high in the air that he thought he'd need a 12 gauge shot gun to bring it down. Needless to say, that pony went into the corral until the next horse sale.

While we were watching the sale ring, in rode this fellow on a big black gelding. He stops, it turns, it backs up, side steps, keeps the rope tight and does all the right things that a good saddle horse should do. To top this all off, he dismounts, taps the horse on the knee and the horse kneels down. Talk about a show!

The bidding was wild but my hand stayed up the longest and we brought Black Prince home. Everyone thought that this was a horse that knew everything and that he was sure going to earn his oats.

The next day I saddled him up and gave him a little run. Low and behold he was wind-broke. This can be caused in a horse if he has been ridden too hard at sometime in his life. He can get the air into his lungs, which have been over expanded, but cannot squeeze his lungs to get the air out again. In the early years some tried tying a sack over their nose to warm the air, but it didn't ever seem to work. To my knowledge there still isn't a cure.

When Black Prince galloped he would wheeze like an old steam engine and could not run any distance. I tried to ease the pain of the cheque that I had cut by thinking off all the good things that he could do, which became pretty small in number, in everyday work life.

Two of his most irritating habits were that he was always in love with another horse, and he was a trailer lover. You could be miles away from the truck and trailer, and he would always be leaning on the bridle rein to head back that way. Some lady told me to tie him up close to the trailer for a day with his head high, and that would cure him.

Another Fairy Tale about horses!

The worst wreck that I had with Prince was during calving season. We had ridden out and of course there was a cow trying to give birth with just one leg and the nose showing. I had just gotten Prince into his fastest gear when he looked sideways at another horse, whinnied, stepped into a hole and stumbled. We both went ass over appetite. No one was hurt, but as we got up I had begun to dislike him, and at that moment it was pretty close to hate.

Another time we were going to move a few yearlings to a little pasture a couple of miles away. I had left the 125 motorbike over at the pasture to check the gates after the move. It was dark when we got there, so I told the girls to ride home and not to worry about Prince, as he would follow them. I jumped on the motorbike, turned on the lights and was checking the gates. When I got out on the road to go home I had to duck my head down to keep the bugs out of my eyes, as the bike had no windshield.

I was purring down the road about 25 miles an hour, when I glanced up for a second. In the headlights, sure enough there was the reflection of a stirrup right in front of my handlebar. Prince had decided to cross the road, and I T-boned him. I don't think that even a trick rider could have timed it more perfect. The wind came out of him that time in a great big whossss and I went flying over the handlebars. I got a pretty bad road rash. Later in the house as I was picking gravel out of my arms and whiskers again I decided that I didn't dislike him. I hated him.

However, you can't abuse an animal for some faults. Besides, we had other plans for him.

We needed Black Prince on the buggy for Grandpa and Grandma to drive in the big Homecoming Parade. He was a saddle horse so we began to drive him on a cart to tame him down and to get him used to the harness.

Everything went well until we tied him up and went to the house for lunch. Something spooked him and he reared up and broke the halter shank and pulled off the bridle and blinders.

He took one look behind and saw the cart following him and was gone in full flight. He went out the east gate at full speed, only the cart didn't make it through. The wheel hit the gatepost and rolled up it about 10 feet and brought Prince to a sliding stop. He spun around under the shaft and took a look at the buggy way up in the air and backed up as quickly as you could blink an eye. In fact he backed right out of the harness, broke the belly band and left the corral with only the collar around his neck, and was gone.

I finally caught him about two hours later and got him calmed down. For months later, he would always shy around the gate -post. That proved the old theory about fright and flight. It was surprising that he could run like he did as he was wind broke and couldn't force the air out of his lungs. Fright can certainly make certain situations funny or very serious.

Prince did himself proud pulling the buggy in the parade. We had him all washed up and polished like a jewel. Grandma and Grandpa were dressed up like rich settlers and they all looked great. When prince got heated up and started to sweat he smelled like a pickle because we had put vinegar in the final rinse to put a beautiful shine on his black coat.

A few weeks after all the Home Coming and hard work, we decided to go for a pack trip in the Rocky Mountains. That was another story, but on this trip Prince turned into the best packhorse out there. He would wiggle by trees and never rub a packsaddle. His only fault was that he was so tall that you had to stand on a stump or a rock to pull the diamond hitch. He was always in love with another horse so you never had to worry about having to tie him, as he would never leave the herd and always followed in single file.

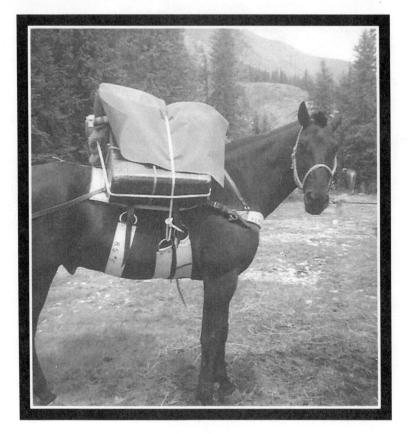

Black Prince

CHAPTER 45
NECKLACE

When you read this title you may think that this will be a nice lady like story however, it is anything but.

My wife and I had been to the rodeo in the Old Edmonton Gardens and it was there that this young brown mare called Necklace fired out of the chutes. Her four white socks and hooves just flashed and shone in the spotlights, as she dashed the dreams of some young cowboy hoping for a pay check or buckle. She eventually bucked herself into the Rodeo Hall of Fame.

I had a saddle mare that just had a foal about a week earlier. When I took the mare and her new colt out for a ride, the colt was feeling pretty frisky and all it wanted to do was buck and leap up into the air. It's four white socks and black shinny hooves just sparkled and flashed in the morning sun. When I came in for coffee I announced that the colt had just named herself. From then on she was Necklace.

Necklace grew up in the freedom of the prairie and short grass country, but she always seemed a little edgy around people. About the time that we should have been starting to train her, we were very busy so I sent her to a horse trainer. That was my first mistake.

After a long time I checked in and said that I needed her back to start working her. I later found out that the trainer hadn't been working her and had taught her very little and had probably got panicky and tried to force train her in a day or so, when it was known that I was coming to pick her up.

When I brought her home she was just sulky, mean, didn't want to run, would jam you in the stall and all those little irritating things. One good thing is that she did load into the trailer nicely, so I took her out to check pastures.

One very hot day we had been going along nicely when I put my arm up to wipe the sweat from my forehead. I don't know if my arm scared her or my hand scraped the brim of my straw hat, but she reared straight up and leaped straight ahead. I didn't have a chance. I kicked free of the stirrups. And went out the back door like snot off a pigs snout.

I lay on the ground awhile, just to make sure that everything worked and then walked a half a mile to catch her. Every step made me madder, so when I caught her I just crawled on her and did the over and under, with the lines for about 15 minutes.

She just ran and never offered to buck.

By the time I got back home I realized that she must have been badly abused and had learned to fight back.

I took her to the round pen and did some Monte Roberts technique on her. It was new to me, on how to read a horse's thoughts and benefit from them. It did turn out according to the book and the clinics I had taken from Monte Roberts down in Las Vegas. The lick and slobber and the way that she looked at me and cocked her ears was a real buzz to anyone that wanted to train a wild horse. It worked well for me, as we did the join up, and we bonded very well. She would got nuts however if anyone else ever tried to tie her up.

She really trusted no one else. I had talked to Monte about her the next time I saw him in Vegas. He wanted my story, but I never did get around to writing it for his magazine.

I had a good summer with Necklace. We Team Penned and I did a bit of roping off her. She grew into a big strong horse, liked to work and was as pretty as a picture.

Some things that happen are nobody's fault, but they just don't turn out for the best. A hunter had stopped by and said, "you know I counted close to 350 Elk on a quarter section of yours out west." I took Necklace and my camera and went out to get some pictures. We had just started out towards the herd of Elk when a flock of partridge blew up, right under her nose. She switched ends so fast on me that I didn't have a chance and landed on my camera and fist right in my ribs. Necklace ran about 20 feet and stood shaking, with her eyes as big as saucers. She knew that something had gone wrong but didn't know what. I talked her down, then got on and rode her back to the truck.

I had a doctor's appointment later that afternoon and was telling him about my experience. He said, "Let me have a feel of those ribs." When he pressed on my ribs they cracked like the sound of breaking a stick. He turned pretty white and said, "you had better get an X-ray." Luckily nothing was broken. I think he had just pushed me back into shape. For years later we would always joke, "just don't press my ribs"

A few weeks later Diane and I were moving some cows around. She was on the Quad A.T.V. and I was riding Necklace again. It was a cold, miserable, windy day and nothing seemed to want to move. I pulled Necklace's head around and gave her a hard kick in the ribs, which I shouldn't have done. She blew high and wide!

Diane thought that I was going to ride her.

I didn't!

After six jumps she threw me so high that I could see the tops of the Neutral Hills. On the way down she hit me with her rump and I flipped over and landed on my head and neck, and was out cold for a while, with blood running from my mouth, nose and ear.

Diane being a nurse felt that I had a punctured a lung, because I was having some trouble breathing. She propped me up against the wheel of the A.T.V. so that I could breathe better. (We were one mile from the house and any other vehicle and she sure wasn't going to get on Necklace to ride home.) She walked and led the horse. Being a true ranchers wife, she even unsaddled the horse and put her in the corral before coming for me.

We went into the hospital and I was wheeled in and x-rayed. The Doctor who was a friend of ours said "I believe you have broken some ribs loose."

Sure enough, he showed us 6 ribs had been broken away from my backbone, plus I had a broken jaw. I slept in a chair for a couple months, because if I tried to lie down the pain was unbearable and I just couldn't breath.

The worst part of it was that everybody in the world had suffered from broken ribs and had to tell me all about them.

The sympathy was overwhelming!

I got a phone call from a fellow who worked in the feedlot and he needed a saddle horse. I couldn't ride for a while, so I explained the situation to him. He came over to get her to go to work.

He just loved her, as she was so willing and smart. She could cut and pen cattle with ease and smoothness all day and he had nothing but good to say about her every time he saw me that winter.

There was a distemper outbreak in the lot. If the distemper breaks outward the horse will live. However if it breaks inward the horse will die very quickly. He left her well and happy in her pen on the Friday night. When he came back Monday she was dead! It was a sad ending for her, but my family was a bit edgy about me riding her again, and I know that I would have had she come home.

Now I often wonder if she had been given a better start in life if her ways would have been different, less violent and aggressive in nature. I can't help but compare her to so many human beings that must spend their life behind bars, because of a harsh beginning.

Necklace

Chapter 46
Stick Horses

Of all the uses for wood I believe that the stick horse played a big part in our western culture. The story that I like to tell is when Grandpa took our two young children berry picking. It was a hot day and they had walked a long way from the truck to the Saskatoon Berry Patch.

As the day wore on they had their lunch and by the time they were ready to walk out again the whining had gotten pretty loud. Grampa stopped and cut a stick horse for each child. Now he said,

"You name them and ride them back to the truck".

You would not believe the fun that they had riding those horses. Time flew by and they were soon back to the truck.

Of course the horses were loaded into the back of the truck and they all headed happily for home.

At a western play one time, out of the bucking chute comes a little cowboy, with a big hat and boots riding his stick horse. This horse reared and bucked hard, did some high dives, swapped ends and the little buckaroo bit the dust. He got up, tipped his hat to the hard bucking stick horse and then swaggered off the stage.

It was a real contest and the crowd loved it.

Always remember: If you get a stick horse always tie him to the porch tightly so he doesn't run away. If you approach him from the backside always let him know were you are or you could get really badly kicked.

A pretty fancy stick horse called Banner

CHAPTER 47
BUDDY

When we sold our ranch and moved down to Okotoks we brought along some good solid ranch horses, and some colts. However, there was nothing that was really reliable for a small child to learn to ride on. We call that type of a horse "Bomb Proof". We now had two little grandkids ready to start to ride. I had always said that it would be nice to make a couple of cowgirls, or cowboys out of them, instead of seeing them hanging around the malls all day.

Like real cowboys….. instead of 7-11 cowboys.

Diane's cousin stopped by one day. He is a long distance trucker and retired saddle bronc rider. He said, "we've got just the pony for you and the cost is nothing!"

His name is Buddy, and he taught a whole family of kids how to ride, then they gave him to us for our Grandkids. They have pretty well outgrown him, and now want faster, and quicker ponies."

They lived in northwestern Alberta. We hooked onto the stock trailer and went to have a look at this horse, knowing full well that he would come home with us.

Buddy had wintered outside with the bulls and mother nature had him well prepared for the cold, as his hair must have been four inches long and very shaggy. He wasn't very big but had a huge head, with a white blaze right down the front. His head looked like a Clydesdale while the rest of him was about the size of a Shetland Pony. His coat was a dirty gray, so he definitely didn't win any beauty contests, but he had the heart of a champion.

No one seemed to know his history, or age ..other than being old. Because he was small and sturdy, I always wondered if his ancestry was the ponies that used to work underground in the coal mines.

Lori told the story about hearing the kids screaming in the yard one day and looked out the window. There was Buddy with the saddle turned underneath him and the kids still clinging to it. He stood there patiently, the look on his face was, "O.K when you get yourselves organized, we can move on!"

We put a halter on him, it took a big one, and led him to the trailer. He kind of stumbled in and looked ready for a new crop of kids to teach.

About a half hour down the road Diane said, "maybe you had better check on him, as I haven't heard a sound, and maybe he is dead!" I checked and he was doing fine …just kind of leaning against the wall for balance.

Diane phoned ahead to our daughter Jodi that was all prepared to bring her excited two little ones out to the ranch to meet Buddy. Our daughter had been in 4-H and was a very good judge of livestock confirmation. We warned her not to expect perfection, and that if she couldn't find nice words to describe him to just say,

"He's awfully cute isn't he?"

We brushed and brushed him and he would roam around the yard and rub on anything and everything to get rid of all his long winter hair. I'll bet you could of stuffed a dozen pillows with all that dead gray hair.

Buddy was everything that you could have wished for the small kids to learn to ride on. I was absolutely amazed how he could sense a child's ability and switch gears from a fast trot to a very slow walk and turning with a sleight touch of a rein. If anyone started to slip, he would just stop and wait for them to get control again, or fall off.

I don't know why, but all the girls and women loved him and they just couldn't keep their hands off him, always cuddling, petting and cooing over him. He certainly wasn't handsome on the outside, but had a beautiful heart and soul.

Our little Granddaughter was in grade two when she had to take something to show and tell. She was hemming and hawing for several days. Finally her mother said, "Tell me, what do you really want to take to show and tell tomorrow?"

Our little blond Granddaughter replied.

"Do you think that Grandpa would bring in Buddy?"

We got a phone call just before bedtime. ..

What could a good Grampa say but yes?

When Jodi went to tell Riley that Grampa would bring Buddy to school tomorrow she was overjoyed, and said,

"You mean he's bringing the real Buddy?"

The arrangements were set up with the teacher.

The next morning we got Buddy all brushed up and loaded in the trailer, and went to Riley's Grade 2 Class in downtown Calgary.

On the way Diane says to me,

"Are we crazy or what! If Buddy acts up or kicks a kid, we'll have our butts sued off, or else the school will."

We unloaded Buddy in the Parking lot. 45 kids poured out of the school to pet him and ask questions. Out of that class only about five had actually ever petted a horse before. They couldn't get over how soft his nose was. There were kids hugging and petting him......
all over!

One was interested how you would put shoes on a horse and, "wouldn't it hurt him?" So it was explained how his hoof was like your fingernail and had no feeling at the end, so could be trimmed and a nail put in where there was no feeling.

With all this attention Buddy was the perfect Gentleman. He wasn't even restless or didn't even poop!

Talk about making a little Granddaughter's day! As an added bonus, her brother was in kindergarten and their class of 30 or more came out for a visit as well. I think that Buddy enjoyed all the petting as much as the kids enjoyed meeting him.

It wasn't unusual to look in our arena and see three little girls riding him. One day Riley had got him to gallop a bit and came running into the house shouting..

"Grandma-Grampa I broke the speed limit today."

You could walk into the barn and there would be his huge head with the blaze face looking out from the stall. Many people thought that we had a big Clydesdale, but would take a look in the stall and there was little Buddy.

I gave him a needle one day for sleeping sickness and he really hated it. He flew out of the barn on his sturdy little legs and he sulked at the far end of the pasture for two days.

Although we never knew his past, he certainly made history at our place for many little kids wanting to ride and to fulfill their dreams of being little cowboys, or cowgirls.

One night he just laid down beside the hay feeder and went to sleep.

The end of an era, but by then thanks to Buddy our grandkids had learned to ride and could now move to the bigger horses.

Buddy & friends

CHAPTER 48

SWAN SONG

Many farming practices have changed since I was a boy. The latest advancement was Zero till, which I was the first to use in our area. When I quit ranching and farming, we had a 57 foot air seeder and a big tractor that burned 17 gallons of diesel fuel per hour. My last year of farming I seeded 5,000 acres of canola all by myself. I would have to stop three times a day to fill up with fertilizer, and once a day to fill up with seed and fuel. You would have coffee and lunch on these stops, and it wasn't too bad at all, with air conditioning and your radio.

We would do a chemical burn off before seeding with a one hundred –foot sprayer. It carried 1200 gallons of water in the spray tank. This outfit was set to go at 10 miles per hour, so you can imagine that when turning the 50 foot outside boom was coming around pretty fast. Not unlike the crack the whip game. You didn't ever want to misjudge the distance on the corners, around the bushes, or near the fence posts.

One man alone can now crop thousands of acres.

With the computer technology and the G.P.S. large machinery, farming is so different and efficient. What remains the same is that you can do everything right and according to the book, but nature can throw a curve at you, over which you have no control. All your years work can suddenly be for naught. If your sole enterprise is grain farming this means that you have no payday for the complete year. Mother nature is still the boss when it comes to a good crop or a failure.

The livestock enterprise has advanced as well with better prevention and treatment of diseases. Improved genetics have brought us faster gains with more efficient cattle.

Rotational grazing and the implementation of swath grazing on our ranch cut down the workload considerably, however, the basic unit is still your cowherd that demands much more individual care and attention. You cannot just turn off the key and come back after the weekend to resume their care.

When I was a sitting member of the Alberta Cattle Commission I always used to tell them that as a Rancher the two things that I enjoyed the most were riding horses and the cheque when you sold your cattle. I always added.

"You'd better have a good saddle horse and enjoy the ride because the cattle cheque may not always be as much as you have hoped for."

Throughout my ranching years, some of the individual personalities of my four legged friends provided me with great amusement and satisfaction. I have found that your horse, your dog, or a special cow can be your best friend and that you can communicate with them on a personal level.

I first attended the Calgary Stampede in the early 1940's when I was very young. My Dad had purchased a second hand car in the spring and he promised us that if the egg and cream prices stayed up that we would make the 250-mile trip to Calgary for the Stampede.

I had never seen a paved road before and Highway #2 seemed like a racetrack to me. There was no air conditioning so the windows were rolled down and the traffic just flew by. We arrived late at night and stayed at a Bed & Breakfast. The next morning we were up bright and early for pancake breakfast and the big parade. It seemed that there was music and square dancing on every corner. The next excitement was going to the big rodeo. I can still recall all the Clown and Bull Fighting acts. It starred Slim Pickens and was quite the experience for a young lad from Metiskow.

I grew up settled down and ranched for over 60 years before retiring south of Calgary. We brought with us my favorite saddle horse Molly who had served me faithfully for nearly 20 years. She was a multi talented cow horse who was always on the bit even after a 12-hour day on the range. She could always catch one more animal and never fell with me once, despite many high-speed maneuvers over the prairie, muskeg, or icy feedlots. She could drag the biggest meanest ugliest bull into a stock trailer after you roped him. She even saved my life a few times while I was treating cows and calves alone on the range. She and I pulled many a calf during the calving seasons.

Down here it seemed that everyone was a cowboy. I have come to the conclusion that cowboys are just ranchers with a little more imagination and talent.

I joined a Riding Club and signed up to ride in the Calgary Stampede Parade using Molly. Quite the experience for us both, being from where our nearest town was 20 miles away and the population was 65 people plus 12 dogs.

The day of the parade we were all decked out and Molly looked her own sharp self, holding her head high and eager to take on the world. To see the tens of thousands of people lining the streets of the parade route was almost overwhelming.

I so enjoyed making eye contact with the seniors and the young children, and saying,

"Howdee"

Molly was a perfect lady and I think she enjoyed the excitement as much as I did.

It was quite the Swan Song for this old Cowboy and his favorite mare Molly.

Molly & I in the Calgary Stampede Parade

Bio
Lorne A. Maull

Lorne and his wife Diane have retired to DeWinton, Alberta, to be near their families. They have known each other for over 55 years, and are still the best of friends. Of course they still have horses, and a dog. Lorne likes to busy himself with many exquisite wood working projects, made from vintage machinery, or other fine woods. He is active in a writers group, and brings much humor, and enthusiasm to the group.

Lorne was born and raised during the depression, on an isolated small farm on the Canadian Prairies. He rode horse back to a one-room school for nine years until the school closed. Becoming a part of the work force at a very early age, he saw much of the heritage farming, and hardships on a very personal level.

He attended the Vermilion School of Agriculture, and later bought a quarter of land, started ranching, and growing this enterprise until it was one of the largest in the area. He always said that he had a short attention span. Lorne was always trying something new, or better to increase production, or to make work easier. He has been a great steward of the land.

Lorne is an excellent stockman, and over the years has had many special saddle horses and stock dogs which were well trained, and loyal to their dedicated master. He always said he had many friends, a lot of whom were four legged. Many a tear was shed at the loss of some of his favorite animal friends.

He has always been a mover and shaker in the Community as well as in various agricultural organizations and 4-H. Lorne is gifted with a sense of humor, which he brings into his many….. hilarious stories of his experiences. He met many real life characters, who became his friends, and he was always eager to hear their stories. It is interesting to ride along with him to meet some of the people that he has known, but most of all to hear about the happenings, at and around the 7 M Running Bar.

Lorne & Diane Maull

The End